100
BEST
GLUTEN-FREE
RECIPES

CAROL FENSTER

PHOTOGRAPHS BY
JAMIE TIAMPO

Houghton Mifflin Harcourt

Boston New York

Copyright © 2010 Carol Fenster

Photos Copyright © 2010 Jamie Tiampo

Published simultaneously in Canada

For information about permission to reproduce selections from this book, please write to Permissions, Houghton Mifflin Harcourt Publishing Company 215 Park Avenue South NY NY 10003.

www.hmhbooks.com

Library of Congress Cataloging-in-Publication Data

Fenster, Carol Lee.
100 best gluten-free recipes / Carol Fenster.
p. cm.
Includes index.
ISBN 978–0–470–47583–6 (cloth)
1. Gluten-free diet—Recipes. I. Title. II. Title: One hundred best gluten-free recipes.
RM237.86.F45 2010
641.5'638—dc22
2009031383

Printed in China

SCP 20 19 18 17 16 15 14 13 12 11 10 9 8
4500418447
Publisher: Natalie Chapman
Senior Editor: Linda Ingroia
Assistant Editor: Charleen Barila
Senior Production Editor: Jacqueline Beach
Cover Design: Suzanne Sunwoo
Interior Design and Layout: Elizabeth Van Itallie
Manufacturing Manager: Kevin Watt

Acknowledgments

I want to thank the staff at Wiley, especially my fabulous editor, Linda Ingroia, who suggested this book and its predecessor, *1,000 Gluten-Free Recipes*, and her talented assistant editor, Charleen Barila. They make a terrific team. I also appreciate the beautiful photographs of my recipes, prepared by food stylist Iri Greco and shot by photographer Jamie Tiampo. Thanks also to Jackie Beach for skillfully shepherding the book from production to printing and to cover designer Suzanne Sunwoo and interior designer Elizabeth Van Itallie for creating such an inviting, beautiful book. And I am grateful for the ongoing support of my friend and marvelous agent, Lisa Ekus-Saffer. I am fortunate to work with many outstanding professional colleagues in the gluten-free community and my readers are the absolute best. I extend my love to my family—Larry, Brett, Helke, Keene, Romi, and Cole— and my gratitude for their support.

Author's Note

The recipes in this book were selected from the award-winning *1,000 Gluten-Free Recipes*, a colossal tome that is the largest gluten-free cookbook ever published; it has everything you need to know and is a great reference. My goal for this smaller but very useful book is to give you the "must-have" recipes—the dishes people ask me for again and again, along with just-what-you-need-to-know information to make the book your go-to guide on a daily basis. You'll find easy-to-follow recipes for breads, desserts, breakfast, snacks, grains, pasta, and vegetables, each one perfect for every day or entertaining. Also, as I am continuously working on new recipes—for classics and trendy foods, new to this book are recipes you'll love, such as Chiles Rellenos, Fresh Chive Flatbread with Dipping Oil, Ice Cream Cones, Cannoli, and a basic sponge cake. I take great pleasure in writing gluten-free cookbooks because they make it possible for gluten-free people to enjoy delicious food, just like everyone else. This gorgeous little book is the perfect gift for your gluten-free friends, family, and of course, for yourself. Bon appétit—without wheat!

Contents

Introduction

To paraphrase a familiar Nashville tune, "I was gluten-free when gluten-free wasn't cool." Having followed the gluten-free lifestyle for over twenty years now, I feel qualified to say if there was ever a time to be gluten-free, it's now. It seems that everyone—the medical profession, university research centers, restaurants, cruise ships, food manufacturers, resorts, natural food stores, supermarkets, and cooking schools—is interested in meeting the needs of this rapidly growing group.

Research by Mintel shows that 8 percent of Americans (about twenty-five million people) shop for gluten-free food, and the number of foods bearing the gluten-free label is somewhere around 3,500—a far cry from the handful of choices we had twenty years ago. Improvements in the quality of gluten-free food, more accurate tests, and a greater willingness of physicians to administer these tests for a food-related condition they once thought was "rare"—plus the increased media attention resulting from these advancements—have fueled this growth. But what does it mean to be gluten-free?

What Is Gluten?

Living gluten-free means avoiding gluten, a naturally occurring protein in wheat and related grains, such as barley, rye, kamut, spelt, and triticale. It is the component of wheat flour that provides wonderful elasticity in bread dough, but can toughen pie crusts and biscuits if the dough is handled too much. (Oats do not contain gluten, but were banished from the gluten-free diet because of possible contamination with wheat in the field or during processing. See The Special Case of Oats on page 14.)

Gluten is in a variety of ingredients and foods, perhaps more than you think. Soups, soup mixes, bouillon, and seasonings, for example, may use wheat as thickeners or for bulk. Licorice candy uses wheat for body. Deli meats or imitation seafood often use wheat as a binder. Barley malt gives flavor to malt vinegar and flavored teas. Salad dressings use wheat flour as a thickener, and it gives both flavor and body to broth.

WHERE IS GLUTEN?

OBVIOUS SOURCES OF GLUTEN

- Bagels
- Breads
- Cakes
- Cereals
- Cookies
- Muffins
- Pancakes
- Pasta
- Tortillas
- Waffles
- Anything made with wheat, and related grains of barley, rye, spelt, kamut, and triticale

SURPRISING SOURCES OF GLUTEN

- Bouillons
- Broths
- Deli meats
- Imitation seafood
- Licorice candy
- Malt vinegar
- Salad dressings
- Seasonings
- Soup and soup mixes
- Tea (flavored)

Who Can't Eat Gluten?

The gluten-free diet is used to treat a variety of medical conditions.

CELIAC DISEASE

Celiac disease is an inherited autoimmune disorder that affects the digestive process of the small intestine. When gluten is eaten, the hairlike cilia that line the small intestine and absorb nutrients from food become inflamed and eventually flatten, thus inhibiting the absorption of important nutrients into the body.

Dr. Alessio Fasano, Medical Director of the Center for Celiac Research at the University of Maryland, says that approximately one in 133 Americans—ten times more than originally thought—has celiac disease and he calls it the "most prevalent genetically transmitted condition in the world." This means that nearly three million Americans are living with this disease, taking an average of eleven years to get a correct diagnosis, according to Dr. Peter Green at Columbia University's Celiac Disease Center.

Unlike many other diseases, there is no pill, no vaccine, and no surgical procedure to cure celiac disease. The only treatment is a lifelong gluten-free diet. If gluten is ingested, the intestines are damaged even if one doesn't experience the typical symptoms of diarrhea, bloating, gas, or fatigue. In fact, experts say that roughly one-third to one-half of celiac patients do not exhibit these typical symptoms.

Celiac disease must be managed with the help of a gastroenterologist, who performs a series of tests––including a small-bowel endoscopy while the patient is sedated––before a final diagnosis is made. For more information on celiac disease, see the Sources section.

ALLERGIES AND INTOLERANCES

According to the Food Allergy & Anaphylaxis Network, about twelve million Americans suffer from true food allergies and wheat is one of the top eight food allergens. There is no single statistic for what portion of this group is truly allergic to wheat, but it is thought to be a small portion of the overall market.

True food allergies involve the immune system's IgE antibodies, and reactions are usually sudden and more pronounced. Few people have true allergies to wheat, but for those who do, it's very serious.

In contrast to the few people with wheat allergies, experts say far more Americans have intolerances to gluten. Unlike true food allergies, the reactions involved in food intolerances involve IgG antibodies. Reactions may be delayed, are usually more subtle, and can take many different forms. Some people––like me–– experience nasal congestion and stuffiness, a feeling of fatigue, and what we ruefully call "brain fog." Others have headaches (sometimes migraines), stomachaches, rashes, achy joints, and a host of other maladies that are as easily associated with other ailments as with a food intolerance. That's why it's often difficult to pinpoint food intolerances.

Diagnosis of a food allergy or intolerance should be made by a board-certified allergist or a health professional that specializes in this area. There are a variety of tests and procedures used to confirm a diagnosis but not all experts agree on a single approach.

AUTISM

According to Autism Speaks, approximately one in 110 children are estimated to have autism, a neurobiological disorder that seems to be rising and perplexes families and the medical community alike. As part of the overall treatment (but not as a substitute for other treatment or as a cure for autism), several experts advocate a gluten-free, casein-free diet (casein is a milk protein). All recipes in this book are also free of dairy, or can be made dairy-free. According to these experts, some autistic children don't process these gluten and milk proteins properly and removing them from the diet helps their behavior. The use of a gluten-free, casein-free diet for autistic children remains controversial and I am not an expert in autism, but many families use my recipes for their autistic children. You and your physician should decide whether this diet is right for your child.

Other medical conditions may warrant a gluten-free diet. For example, people with food-triggered asthma are sometimes placed on gluten-free diets. Some physicians recommend a gluten-free diet as part of the treatment (but not a cure) for certain autoimmune conditions. You should rely on the advice of your physician as to whether a gluten-free diet is appropriate for you.

How to Use This Book

This book of one hundred recipes is divided into five chapters: Breakfasts, Breads, and Muffins; Soups, Salads, and Snacks; Grains, Beans, and Pasta; Main Dishes; and Desserts. Within each chapter, you'll find a wide selection of recipes that are perfect for everyday meals or entertaining, with special icons indicating which recipes are Vegetarian (no meat or dairy) 🦃, Quick (30 minutes or less to prepare) 🕐, and Kids' Favorite ☺ —that is, foods kids like.

Read this introduction thoroughly before you start cooking; it tells you where gluten lurks, which ingredients to stock in a gluten-free pantry, information on flours and grains in these recipes, and which gluten-free brands were used in developing the recipes. It also explains how to measure ingredients correctly, which is critical to success in gluten-free baking.

The recipe chapters also include helpful sidebars that further explain certain ingredients or offer tips for success with particular recipes. As a bonus, gluten-free menus for a variety of occasions, ranging from everyday to special occasions, are provided. The back of the book lists helpful Web sites for more information on the diet, medical conditions, labeling, foods, dining out, travel, research, testing, and many other things you might want to know about the gluten-free diet.

SAFETY IN THE GLUTEN-FREE KITCHEN

So you've spent lots of time carefully choosing safe ingredients in the grocery store. But it's just as important to handle those ingredients safely at home to assure that they remain gluten-free. Here are just a few of the precautions that will increase the safety of your food.

- Use separate knives, cutting boards, and serving utensils for gluten-free foods. A knife used to spread butter on wheat bread can transfer wheat particles back to the butter. Wheat bread can leave crumbs on a cutting board and contaminate gluten-free bread cut on the same board.

- Use separate appliances when there is the possibility of cross contamination. For example, wheat bread crumbs in a toaster may touch gluten-free toast. Food residue can collect in crevices such as in bread machines (usually where the kneading blade inserts). The same is true for blenders (the area where the blade attaches) or electric mixers (the area where the beaters insert into the mixer).

- Try to minimize particles of wheat flour in the air when sifting or measuring. Carefully wipe down all kitchen surfaces after baking with wheat flour (or regular oats, barley, spelt, or rye) to remove any particles.

- Store gluten-free food in clearly marked, tightly sealed containers on shelves or areas designated as gluten-free to minimize accidental ingestion.

These situations may seem harmless because they involve such small particles or crumbs, but keep in mind that even tiny amounts can make people sick, especially if several unsafe practices accumulate over the course of a day.

THE GLUTEN-FREE PANTRY

When you're new to the gluten-free diet, deciding what to stock in your pantry can seem perplexing. First, check out the recipes in this book and decide which ones you want to make and the ingredients they require. Then, look over the lists in Brands for Gluten-Free, Dairy-Free Ingredients (page 16) and also the lists in Flours and Grains Used in This Book (page 12) for the brands I used in testing these recipes. If you keep those items on hand, you'll always be ready to cook. In addition, here are some basics you will always need to keep on hand:

- xanthan gum and guar gum for baking
- active dry yeast for baking
- baking soda and baking powder for baking
- salt, freshly ground black pepper, and other spices for seasoning
- pickles, ketchup, mayonnaise, mustard, relish, apple cider vinegar
- canned or frozen fruits and vegetables
- canned or dried beans and legumes
- perishables such as eggs, milk, juices, salad greens, fruit, and vegetables

FLOURS AND GRAINS USED IN THIS BOOK

All of the recipes in this book avoid gluten by using gluten-free ingredients. If you're new to the gluten-free lifestyle, you might be unfamiliar with some of the gluten-free flours, grains, and seeds. Many "grains" are actually seeds of plants but we call them grains for simplicity and some flours are ground from vegetables or beans, instead of grains. To add further confusion, sometimes they're used as whole grains, sometimes the whole grains are ground into flours for baking, and sometimes certain grains are used in both ways, that is whole or as flour. There is a quick overview for you on the next page. See Ingredients under Sources on page 188 for companies that provide gluten-free flours and grains.

GRAINS AND FLOURS

	DESCRIPTION	AVAILABLE AS
Almond meal	Ground from whole almonds.	Whole (nut) or flour/meal
Amaranth	Ancient grain once grown by the Aztecs for its superior nutrients. Related to pigweed.	Whole grain or flour
Brown rice	Unpolished whole rice kernel, including bran, germ, and endosperm. When polished, becomes white rice. Whole grain or flour	Whole grain or flour
Buckwheat	Not wheat, but the seed of a plant related to rhubarb. Toasted buckwheat groats are called kasha.	Whole grain or flour
Cornmeal (yellow)	Meal ground from whole corn kernels. Corn flour can also be ground from whole corn kernels.	Flour or meal
Cornstarch	Ground from corn and used as flour to lighten baked goods or as thickener for sauces, gravies, and soups.	Flour
Hemp seed	Easily digested, high-protein hulled seeds; added to baked goods like nuts or ground into protein powder for smoothies.	Whole (nut) or powder (powder can also be used as flour in baking)
Montina	Seed of Indian ricegrass grown in the northwestern U.S. High protein and fiber content; tastes and looks like dark wheat germ.	Flour (sold as pure supplement or mixed with other flours in blend)
Millet	Seed of a grass related to sorghum. Prized for its easily digested (alkaline) protein.	Whole grain or flour
(Gluten-free) Oats* (groats)	Whole oat kernels; no bran removed. (If the bran is removed, it is sold as oat bran. If the whole oat groat is chopped, it is sold as steel-cut oats.)	Whole grain or flour

	DESCRIPTION	AVAILABLE AS
Gluten-free Oats* (rolled)	Whole oat kernel steamed and flattened (rolled) and commonly used to make breakfast oatmeal.	Whole grain
Potato starch	Ground from peeled, dried potatoes. Used to lighten baked goods and thicken sauces and soups.	Flour
Quinoa	Called "mother" grain due to its superior nutrients; ancient grain once cultivated by Incas in Peru. Related to spinach.	Whole grain or flour
Rice bran	Outer hull from brown rice kernel and used in foods for its high fiber and protein.	Rice bran particles or flour
Sorghum	World's fifth largest cereal; seed of a grass common in Asian and Africa but also grown in central U.S. Distantly related to maize.	Whole grain or flour
Sweet rice flour	Ground from white sticky rice (sometimes called glutinous rice) but contains no wheat gluten. Grains often used in sushi. Flour adds pliability to baked goods; excellent thickener for soup.	Whole grain or flour
Tapioca	Ground from manioc or cassava root and adds "chew" and crustiness in baked goods.	Whole grain (tapioca granules to make pudding) or flour.
Teff	Teff, a cereal grass, means "tiny" and comes from Ethiopia, where it is a staple and often used in injera bread.	Whole grain or flour
Wild rice	Not rice, but the seed of an aquatic grass commonly grown in the northern United States.	Whole grain or flour

*Check with your physician before using gluten-free oats.

THE SPECIAL CASE OF OATS

You may be surprised to see oats on the list of grains and flours used in this book. Long off-limits for the gluten-free diet because of contamination with wheat in the field or during processing, several manufacturers now offer oats that are pure and uncontaminated by wheat. Various companies offer these gluten-free oats in the form of whole oat groats (kernels), rolled oats for oatmeal, steel-cut oats for extra-hearty hot cereal, and oat bran and oat flour for baking. Dr. Peter Green of Columbia University says all but 2 percent of the population can safely eat oats, but check with your physician before you try them just in case you're in that 2 percent who don't tolerate them.

These recipes rely on Carol's Sorghum Blend, an extremely versatile blend of flours that can be used as the basis for many dishes. If you keep the following blend in your pantry, you'll always be prepared to bake whenever the need arises.

CAROL'S SORGHUM BLEND

MAKES 4 CUPS

1 ½ cups sorghum flour
1 ½ cups potato starch or cornstarch
1 cup tapioca flour

Whisk the ingredients together until well blended. Store, tightly covered, in a dark, dry place for up to 3 months. You may refrigerate or freeze the blend, but bring to room temperature before using. You may double or triple the recipe.

MEASURING FOR SUCCESS

It is very important to measure gluten-free flours carefully. All the recipes in my books measure flour this way: Whisk the flour a few times to aerate or fluff it up and then lightly spoon it into a measuring cup before leveling it off with a knife. Don't use the measuring cup as a scoop and don't pack the flour down; you'll get up to 20 percent more flour that way, which can adversely affect your baking. Use spouted measuring cups only for liquids like milk and water because it's hard to determine an accurate amount of flour in them.

I use standard brands of flours, such as those from Bob's Red Mill, Ener-G, Authentic Foods, or NuWorld Amaranth, purchased in natural food stores or supermarkets. I don't use superfine flours, such as those from Asian markets, since they are denser and they absorb liquids differently than the standard brands.

SAVVY LABEL READING

It is very important to choose gluten-free ingredients carefully. The Food Allergen Labeling and Consumer Protection Act of 2004 (FALCPA) makes shopping easier because the words Contains: Wheat must appear on any food that contains wheat. But it is extremely important to read the labels each time you buy because manufacturers can change procedures or ingredients at any time and complying with gluten-free requirements is voluntary. A company doesn't have to offer a food without wheat if it doesn't want to. But, again, if it uses wheat the label must say so. Also, the law only requires the warning about wheat (and spelt, which is a form of wheat), not the other gluten-containing grains like barley, rye, kamut, triticale, or non-gluten-free oats— but they will be in the ingredient list so you will know if that food is safe or not.

To further help you identify safe foods, the Gluten-Free Certification Organization (a branch of the Gluten Intolerance Group) certifies companies as gluten-free and authorizes them to display a certification logo on the food item, as does the Celiac Sprue Association and the National Foundation for Celiac Awareness. Companies that don't use these logos don't necessarily manufacture unsafe foods, but these logos are yet another tool for you to use when you shop.

BRANDS FOR GLUTEN-FREE, DAIRY-FREE INGREDIENTS

To help you locate gluten-free, dairy-free versions of certain ingredients, here is a list of the brands I used in testing these recipes. I confirmed their gluten-free status by checking with the manufacturer. You may also find other gluten-free brands in your region. Be sure to always read the label since manufacturers may change ingredients or manufacturing practices, which could change the gluten-free status of a food or ingredient.

GLUTEN-FREE, DAIRY-FREE INGREDIENTS

FOOD OR INGREDIENT	GLUTEN-FREE BRAND(S)
Baking	
Almond paste	Love'n Bake
Bittersweet chocolate	Scharffen Berger
Chia	Navitas
Chocolate chips	Tropical Source
Semisweet/bittersweet chocolate	Tropical Source
White chocolate bar	Vegan Organica
Marshmallow cream	Jet-Puffed by Kraft
Rice bran	Ener-G
Salba	Salba
Shortening (nonhydrogenated)	Earth Balance
Shortening (white)	Spectrum All-Vegetable
Beverages	
Amaretto	De Kuyper
Beer	Bard's Tale, Green's, New Grist, Redbridge, Ramapo Valley, New Planet
Crème de menthe	De Kuyper
Pernod Ricard	Pernod Ricard
Hard cider	Woodchuck Granny Smith
Marsala	Taylor
Orange liqueur	Cointreau or Triple-Sec
Cookies, Breads, and Crackers	
Bread	Glutino, Kinnikinnick, Whole Foods
Breadsticks	Glutino
Cookies	Pamela's (all flavors)
Crackers	Blue Diamond, Edward & Sons, Mary's Gone Crackers
Pretzels	Ener-G or Glutino
Tortilla (or tortilla wraps)	Food for Life, La Tortilla Factory, Rudi's
White bread	Whole Foods
Broth, Canned Goods, Condiments, Seasonings, and Spices	
Asian fish sauce	Taste of Thai
Beef broth	Kitchen Basics, Swanson's
Chicken broth	Kitchen Basics, Swanson's Natural Goodness

FOOD OR INGREDIENT	GLUTEN-FREE BRAND(S)
Broth, Canned Goods, Condiments, Seasonings, and Spices, cont.	
Creole seasoning	Spice Hunter
Marinara sauce	Classico, Prego
Mexican salsa	Newman's Own, Pace, or Tostito
Red chile sauce	Las Palmas
Seasoned salt	Lawry's
Thai green curry paste	Thai Kitchen
Wheat-free tamari soy sauce	San-J
Worcestershire sauce	French's
Dairy Products	
Buttery spread	Earth Balance or Soy Garden
Cream cheese	Vegan Gourmet or Tofutti
Nonfat dry milk powder	Better Than Milk soy powder
Almond milk	Almond Breeze
Hazelnut milk	Pacific Natural Foods
Hemp milk	Living Harvest
Potato milk	Vance's Dari-Free
Rice milk	Rice Dream
Soy milk	Silk
Cheese Alternatives	
Parmesan	Soyco
Monterey Jack, Cheddar	Vegan Gourmet, Daiya
Meat	
Black Forest Ham	Boar's Head
Hot dogs	Applegate Farms
Pepperoni	Applegate Farms, Hormel
Sausage (Andouille)	Applegate Farms
Crabmeat	Phillips
Cocktail franks	Thumann's
Pasta	
Elbow macaroni, fettuccine, penne, spaghetti	Tinkyada

Menus

Wondering how to assemble the recipes in this cookbook into menus? Here are some ideas for every day and special occasions.

Spring Has Sprung
Penne Pasta Primavera
Caesar Salad with Croutons
French Yeast Bread
Strawberry Pie with Whipped Cream

Veggie, Please
Grilled Vegetables on Brown Rice
Fresh Chive Flatbread with Dipping Oil
Flourless Dark Chocolate Cake

All-American Supper
Chicken-Fried Chicken with White Gravy
Mashed potatoes
Vegetables of your choice
Cherry Cobbler

For Kids of All Ages
Corn Dogs
Macaroni and Cheese
Fresh vegetables of your choice
Ice Cream Cones

Elegant Dinner Party
Crab Cakes (miniature for appetizers)
Pan-Grilled Rosemary Lamb Chops
Orange-Scented Wild Rice with Dried Fruits
Beet-Orange Salad with Crispy Goat Cheese Rounds
Rustic Nectarine Frangipane Tart

Weekend Brunch
Sun-Dried Tomato Quiche or Breakfast Egg and Cheese Strata
Cheese Blintzes with Cherries or Buttermilk Crumb Coffee
  Cake
Fresh fruit of your choice

Down South
Shrimp Étouffée
Hush Puppies
Individual Fruit Tarts in Coconut Crusts

Southwestern
Pork Carnitas in a Slow Cooker
Black or pinto beans of your choice
Frozen Margarita Pie

Italian Dinner
Spaghetti with Meatballs
Focaccia with Herbs
Mixed green salad of your choice
Tiramisù

Asian Influence
Pan-Fried Grouper in Thai Curry Sauce
Vegetable Tempura with Dipping Sauce
Store-bought coconut sorbet

BREAKFASTS, BREADS, AND MUFFINS

BREAKFASTS
Gluten-Free Naked Granola
Breakfast Egg and Cheese Strata
Cheese Blintzes with Cherries
Buttermilk Pancakes
Basic Bacon and Cheese Quiche

QUICK BREADS AND MUFFINS
Hush Puppies
Cornbread
Buttermilk Biscuits
Irish Soda Bread
Herb Popovers
Banana Bread
Old-Fashioned Molasses Quick Bread
Cranberry-Orange Scones with Orange Glaze
Chocolate Chip Muffins with White Chocolate Drizzle
Basic Muffins with Streusel Topping

YEAST BREADS
White Sandwich Yeast Bread
High-Fiber Bran Yeast Bread
Light Rye Beer Yeast Bread
Cinnamon Raisin Yeast Bread
French Yeast Bread
Pumpernickel French Yeast Bread
Pepperoni Pizza
Soft Pretzels
Focaccia with Herbs
Fresh Chive Flatbread with Dipping Oil
Breadsticks

Gluten-Free Naked Granola

MAKES 4 CUPS

This is a simple, lightly sweetened yet tasty version of granola. Without the "lumps and bumps" of nuts and fruit it is "naked," and you can personalize it for piecrusts, toppings for fruit crisps, or as a base for trail mixes for the kids. For a sweeter granola, increase the honey to ½ cup.

3 cups gluten-free rolled oats*
I cup raw natural coconut or sweetened coconut flakes
I teaspoon ground cinnamon
¼ teaspoon salt
⅓ cup honey
¼ cup boiling water
¼ cup canola oil
I teaspoon pure vanilla extract

1. Place a rack in the middle of the oven. Preheat the oven to 300°F. Line a 15 × 10-inch baking sheet (not nonstick) with parchment paper or lightly coat with cooking spray.

2. In a large bowl, place the oats, coconut, cinnamon, and salt and toss to thoroughly combine.

3. In a small bowl, combine the liquid ingredients and stir until the honey is dissolved. Pour over the dry ingredients and toss with a rubber spatula until thoroughly combined. (The mixture will be fairly wet and look very glossy.) Place the granola on the prepared sheet and spread to a thin layer.

4. Bake 15 minutes and stir. Bake another 15 minutes and stir again. Continue baking in 10-minute increments until the granola is golden brown, or browned to the desired degree. Cool the granola in the pan on a wire rack for 20 minutes. Refrigerate, tightly sealed, in a food storage bag or container, up to 2 weeks, or on your pantry shelf for up to I week.

* Check with your physician before using gluten-free oats.

CHEWY GRANOLA BARS

MAKES 24 BARS

¼ cup unsalted butter or buttery spread, at room temperature
¼ cup honey
¼ cup packed light brown sugar
I teaspoon pure vanilla extract
2 cups Gluten-Free Naked Granola (page 21)
I cup Perky's Nutty Flax cereal
½ teaspoon ground cinnamon
½ teaspoon xanthan gum
¼ teaspoon salt
¼ cup gluten-free semisweet chocolate chips

1. In a medium saucepan, combine the butter, honey, and sugar. Bring to a boil over high heat and cook, stirring, until the sugar is melted. Remove from the heat and stir in the vanilla.

2. Stir in the granola, flax cereal, cinnamon, xanthan gum, and salt with a wooden spoon until blended. Then stir in the chocolate chips. Spread in a 13 x 9-inch ungreased glass baking dish. Refrigerate 2 hours or until firm.

MAKING GRANOLA INTO TRAIL MIX

Add ½ cup whole almonds, ¼ cup dried bananas, ¼ cup dark raisins, ¼ cup finely chopped dried apricots, and ½ cup gluten-free semi-sweet chocolate chips. Store in a dark, dry, slightly cool place for up to I week.

COOKED WHOLE GRAINS FOR BREAKFAST

Living gluten-free doesn't mean giving up cereal, which is usually wheat-based. These healthy, gluten-free whole grains cook up into marvelous hot cereals. If these grains are new to you, see page 12, for more information.

Cooking times vary by the age of the grains, their moisture content, and the height and depth of your pot. If the grains are not done when the allotted time is up, add a little more water and continue cooking, always with a lid.

You may add salt and vanilla as the grains cook. Jazz them up for the kids by adding cinnamon, honey, maple syrup, brown sugar, fresh fruit, jam, jelly, or applesauce.

GRAIN (1 CUP)	WATER	COOKING TIME	YIELD
Amaranth	2 cups	15 to 20 minutes	3½ cups
Brown rice	2½ cups	30 to 45 minutes	3½ to 4 cups
Buckwheat (kasha)	1 cup	15 to 20 minutes	4 cups
Millet	2½ to 4 cups	35 to 40 minutes	4 cups
Gluten-free oat groats*	3 cups	35 to 40 minutes	4 cups
Quinoa	2 cups	15 to 20 minutes	3 cups
Sorghum (soak overnight)	2 cups	45 to 60 minutes	3 cups
Wild rice	4 cups	40 minutes	3½ to 4 cups

* Check with your physician before using gluten-free oats.

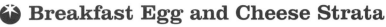

Breakfast Egg and Cheese Strata

MAKES 8 SERVINGS

This dish is perfect for entertaining because you assemble it the day before, refrigerate it overnight, and bake it the next day while you're preparing the rest of the meal. For added flavor, replace ¼ cup of the milk with your favorite dry white wine. This recipe is a great way to use up hard or stale bread.

10 slices White Sandwich Yeast Bread (page 48) or other gluten-free white bread, cut into 1-inch cubes
2 cups Canadian-style bacon, finely diced
2 cups coarsely grated Gruyère or cheese alternative (about 6 ounces)
1 cup finely grated Parmesan cheese or cheese alternative
½ cup store-bought basil pesto
2 tablespoons extra-virgin olive oil
2 tablespoons grated onion or 1 tablespoon dried minced onion
4 large eggs
3 cups milk of choice
1 tablespoon Dijon mustard
1 teaspoon salt
½ teaspoon freshly ground black pepper
¼ teaspoon freshly grated nutmeg
2 tablespoons coarsely chopped fresh flat-leaf parsley

1. Generously grease a 13 × 9-inch baking dish; set aside.

2. In a large bowl, place the bread cubes, bacon, Gruyère, and ¾ cup of the Parmesan; toss until thoroughly combined. In a small bowl, combine the pesto, oil, and onion, and toss with the bread until thoroughly blended. Spread the mixture evenly in the bottom of the prepared baking dish.

3. In the same large bowl, whisk together the eggs, milk, mustard, salt, pepper, and nutmeg and pour evenly over the bread cubes. Cover with plastic wrap and refrigerate overnight.

4. Place a rack in the middle of the oven. Preheat the oven to 350°F. Remove the plastic wrap from the baking dish and sprinkle the strata with the remaining ¼ cup Parmesan. Bake until the top of the casserole is brown, 45 minutes to 1 hour. Let stand 5 minutes before serving. Sprinkle with the parsley and serve.

 Cheese Blintzes with Cherries

MAKES 8 BLINTZES

Cheese blintzes, with their sweet topping, are perfect for brunch or dessert. This versatile crêpe recipe can also be used for savory dishes as well.

CRÊPES
- ¾ cup milk of choice
- ⅔ cup Carol's Sorghum Blend (page 14)
- 2 large eggs
- 6 teaspoons unsalted butter or buttery spread, melted, or canola oil
- ¼ teaspoon xanthan gum
- ⅛ teaspoon salt
- Additional butter, buttery spread, or canola oil, for frying

FILLING
- 1 cup ricotta cheese or firm silken tofu
- 1 small (3-ounce) package cream cheese or cream cheese alternative, at room temperature
- 3 tablespoons powdered sugar, plus ½ cup, for dusting
- Grated zest of 1 lemon
- 1 large egg, at room temperature
- 1 (20-ounce) can cherry pie filling

1. Make the crêpes: In a blender, combine all the ingredients except the additional butter for frying, and process until the mixture is smooth. Just before frying the crêpes, blend again to reincorporate the ingredients.

2. Heat an 8-inch skillet or seasoned crêpe pan over medium-high heat until a drop of water dances on the surface. Brush the surface with butter.

3. For each crêpe, pour a scant ¼ cup batter into the pan and immediately tilt and swirl the pan to coat the bottom evenly with batter. Cook until the underside of the crêpe is crispy brown, then flip the crêpe with a thin spatula and cook the other side until the batter sets, about 20 to 30 seconds. (The first crêpe will often not cook as well as succeeding crêpes until the pan reaches the right temperature.) Stack the cooked crêpes between sheets of aluminum foil, plastic wrap, or parchment paper to prevent drying out. Repeat with the remaining batter.

4. Place a rack in the middle of the oven. Preheat the oven to 400°F. Coat a 13 × 9-inch glass baking dish with cooking spray.

(continued on following page)

5. Make the filling: In a medium bowl, beat the ricotta and cream cheese together with an electric mixer on medium speed until smooth. Gradually beat in the 3 tablespoons sugar, lemon zest, and egg until smooth. Spoon ¼ cup of the cheese mixture in a line along the lower third of each crêpe. Fold the bottom edge away from you to just cover the cheese filling; then fold the 2 sides into the center. Roll the crêpe away from you a couple of times to make a tight package, ending with the seam side down. Place the filled crêpes in the prepared baking dish.

6. Bake until the egg is cooked and the cheese sets, 10 to 15 minutes. Using a spatula, transfer the blintzes to serving plates. Dust with powdered sugar, spoon the cherry pie filling on top, and serve warm.

CHEESE BLINTZES with ASSORTED FRUITS

In step 6, replace the cherry pie filling with apple, apricot, blackberry, or blueberry pie filling.

☺ Buttermilk Pancakes

MAKES 4 LARGE PANCAKES

Serve these easy pancakes with butter and maple syrup, fresh fruit, or your favorite jam or jelly. For kid-size pancakes, use 2 tablespoons of batter per pancake.

1 cup Carol's Sorghum Blend (page 14)
2 tablespoons sugar
1 teaspoon baking powder
½ teaspoon baking soda
¼ teaspoon salt
¼ teaspoon xanthan gum
½ cup buttermilk or Homemade Buttermilk (page 29), well shaken, or more as needed
2 tablespoons unsalted butter or buttery spread, melted, or canola oil
1 large egg
1 teaspoon pure vanilla extract
Additional butter, buttery spread, or canola oil, for frying

1. In a medium bowl or large measuring cup, sift together the sorghum blend, sugar, baking powder, baking soda, salt, and xanthan gum.

2. Gradually whisk in the buttermilk, butter, egg, and vanilla until very smooth. Let the batter stand 5 minutes and then adjust the consistency, with additional buttermilk, if needed (see Tips for Perfect Pancakes, page 29).

3. In a large nonstick (gray, not black) skillet, heat the butter over medium-high heat until hot but not smoking. Pour ¼ cup batter onto the skillet and cook until bubbles appear on top of the pancake, about 2 to 3 minutes. Turn and cook until browned on the other side, about 1 to 2 minutes more. Serve immediately.

(continued on following page)

HOMEMADE BUTTERMILK

MAKES 1 CUP

Rice milk or potato milk will not thicken, so reduce the amount of rice or potato-based buttermilk in recipes by 25 percent. Be sure to shake or whisk the buttermilk well before measuring because the solids tend to settle at the bottom, making the first few cups thinner and the final few cups thicker.

1 tablespoon apple cider vinegar or fresh lemon juice
1 cup milk of choice

Put the vinegar in a measuring cup. Whisk in enough milk to equal 1 cup. Let stand 10 minutes to thicken slightly. Refrigerate the unused portion, tightly covered, for up to 1 week.

TIPS FOR PERFECT PANCAKES

• Let the pancake batter stand 5 minutes before frying the pancakes. This gives the liquid and dry ingredients time to meld and reach the proper consistency.

• Always start with a smaller amount of milk. If the batter looks too thick, add another 2 to 3 tablespoons milk to reach the desired consistency. The batter should be thick enough to spread only slightly when it hits the hot griddle, yet not so thick that it doesn't spread at all. If it spreads very rapidly, add more sorghum blend 1 tablespoon at a time.

• Browning time will vary with the ingredients in your pancake batter, but generally the pancakes are ready to be turned when bubbles start to appear on the surface of the batter. You can also determine if the underside is browned enough to turn by gently lifting the pancake with a spatula and taking a peek. Frying a "test" pancake is always a good idea to see if the skillet heat and the pancake batter are correctly calibrated.

Basic Bacon and Cheese Quiche

MAKES 4 SERVINGS

Quiche is a great choice for an elegant brunch, lunch, or a light dinner. Pair it with a tossed green salad and some crusty French bread (see page 55) for a delightful meal. Keep a few piecrusts rolled out and stored flat in your freezer, and this quiche will go together quickly.

Basic Pastry Crust for a 9-inch single-crust pie (page 168)
I large onion, thinly sliced
3 slices uncooked bacon, cut into I-inch pieces
4 large eggs
¾ cup heavy cream or whole milk of choice
I teaspoon Dijon mustard
I tablespoon sweet rice flour or potato starch
¼ teaspoon salt
⅛ teaspoon freshly grated nutmeg
⅛ teaspoon white pepper
I½ cups diced Swiss cheese or cheese alternative
¼ cup grated Parmesan cheese or cheese alternative

1. Place a rack in the bottom position and another rack in the middle position of the oven. Preheat the oven to 400°F. Fit the piecrust into a 9-inch pie pan and flute the edges, as directed on page 169; set aside.

2. In a heavy skillet, cook the onion and bacon together over medium heat, stirring constantly, until the bacon is crisp and the onion is tender. Transfer the onion and bacon to drain on paper towels and set aside.

3. In a medium bowl, whisk together the eggs, cream, mustard, rice flour, salt, nutmeg, and pepper. Stir in the cooked onion and bacon. Toss the cheeses together and add to the mixture. Pour the mixture into the prepared crust.

4. Bake on the bottom rack of the oven for 15 minutes. Then move the quiche to the middle rack, cover with a sheet of aluminum foil, and continue baking until the quiche is set and a knife inserted in the center comes out clean, about 30 minutes. Serve immediately.

SUN-DRIED TOMATO QUICHE

In step 3, omit the nutmeg and stir in 1½ teaspoons coarsely chopped fresh thyme or ½ teaspoon dried thyme and ½ cup finely diced sun-dried tomatoes. Bake as directed.

SAUSAGE AND LEEK QUICHE

In step 2, replace the bacon with two links of gluten-free sausage, thinly sliced. Replace the onion with two thoroughly cleaned and rinsed, thinly sliced leeks (white parts only).

☺ Hush Puppies

MAKES 10 HUSH PUPPIES

Hush puppies are deep-fried, crispy cornmeal delights—part cornbread and part fritter. They are very simple to prepare and best eaten right after they're made. Make the smaller sizes for the kids.

1½ cups gluten-free yellow cornmeal
½ cup Carol's Sorghum Blend (page 14)
2 teaspoons baking powder
1 tablespoon sugar
½ teaspoon salt
1 small onion, finely chopped
1 large egg, beaten
⅓ to ½ cup milk of choice
Peanut oil, for frying

1. In a small bowl, whisk together the cornmeal, sorghum blend, baking powder, sugar, and salt until thoroughly blended.

2. Whisk in the onion and egg and enough of the milk to form a stiff batter.

3. In a deep pot, heat 3 inches of the oil to 365°F, or use an electric deep-fryer, following the manufacturer's directions. For regular-size hush puppies, drop tablespoonfuls of the batter into the hot oil and fry until they're golden brown, about 3 to 4 minutes. For larger hush puppies, use heaping tablespoons of batter. Remove the hush puppies with a slotted spoon and drain on paper towels. Serve immediately.

 # Cornbread

MAKES 12 SERVINGS

Serve this easy cornbread as a savory bread, or drizzle it with honey and butter for a sweet treat. Make muffins for the kids (see below). You can also add cheese, green chiles, or cooked pancetta for variety. Use leftover cornbread to make stuffing for pork chops or the holiday turkey.

2 large eggs, at room temperature
¾ cup milk of choice, at room temperature
¼ cup canola oil
1 tablespoon apple cider vinegar or fresh lemon juice
1 cup gluten-free yellow cornmeal
¾ cup Carol's Sorghum Blend (page 14)
¼ to ⅓ cup sugar
2 teaspoons baking powder
1½ teaspoons xanthan gum
1 teaspoon salt

1. Place a rack in the middle of the oven. Preheat the oven to 350°F. Generously grease an 8-inch square nonstick (gray, not black) baking dish.

2. In a medium bowl, beat the eggs with an electric mixer on low speed until light yellow and frothy, about 30 seconds. Add the milk, oil, and cider vinegar and beat on low speed until well blended.

3. In a small bowl, whisk together the sorghum blend, sugar, baking powder, xantham gum, and salt. With the mixer on low speed, gradually beat the flour mixture into the liquid ingredients until thoroughly blended. The batter should be the consistency of thick cake batter. Spread the batter evenly in the prepared baking dish

4. Bake until the cornbread is firm and the edges are lightly browned, 25 to 30 minutes. Cool the bread in the pan on a wire rack for 10 minutes. Serve warm.

CORNBREAD MUFFINS

Generously grease a standard 12-cup nonstick (gray, not black) muffin pan or line with paper liners. Divide the batter evenly among the cups and bake until the muffins are lightly browned and firm to the touch, 20 to 25 minutes. Cool in the pan on a wire rack for 5 minutes and then remove from the pan and cool on a wire rack for 5 to 10 more minutes. Serve slightly warm.

☺ Buttermilk Biscuits

MAKES 10 TO 12 BISCUITS

Biscuits are one of the easiest and quickest gluten-free breads to make and can be served hot from the oven—slathered with butter and jam. This ultra-soft, basic biscuit dough—which can be modified for lunch or dinner by adding cheese, bacon bits, or your favorite fresh herbs—is dusted with white rice flour to make it manageable while cutting.

White rice flour, for dusting and rolling
¾ cup Carol's Sorghum Blend (page 14)
¾ cup potato starch
4 teaspoons sugar
1 tablespoon baking powder
1 teaspoon xanthan gum
1 teaspoon guar gum
½ teaspoon baking soda
½ teaspoon salt
¼ cup shortening
1 cup buttermilk or Homemade Buttermilk (page 29), well shaken and at room temperature
2 tablespoons milk of choice or heavy cream, for brushing

1. Place a rack in the middle of the oven. Preheat the oven to 375°F. Generously grease a 13 x 9-inch nonstick (gray, not black) baking sheet or line with parchment paper. Dust the surface lightly with rice flour.

2. In a food processor, pulse together the sorghum blend, potato starch, sugar, baking powder, xanthan gum, guar gum, baking soda, and salt until thoroughly mixed. Add the shortening and buttermilk and process just until the dough forms a ball, scraping down the sides with a rubber spatula, if necessary. The dough will be very, very soft and much stickier than traditional biscuit dough.

3. Place the dough on the baking sheet. Lightly dust the dough with rice flour to facilitate handling. Gently pat the dough to a 1-inch-thick circle. Cut into 10 biscuits, 2 inches in diameter, with a floured metal biscuit cutter. For better rising, push the biscuit cutter straight down on the dough rather than twisting it while cutting. Pat the remaining dough to 1 inch thick and cut again, lightly dusting with white rice flour to prevent sticking, if necessary. Arrange the biscuits evenly on the prepared baking sheet and gently brush the biscuit tops with milk.

4. Bake until the biscuits are nicely browned and crisp, 12 to 15 minutes. Serve immediately.

 Irish Soda Bread

MAKES 10 SERVINGS

Irish soda bread is ideal for those who avoid yeast because it is leavened with baking soda and baking powder instead. It makes great sandwiches, and it can be toasted for breakfast.

2 cups Carol's Sorghum Blend (page 14)
3 tablespoons sugar
1 teaspoon baking soda
1 teaspoon baking powder
1½ teaspoons xanthan gum
1 teaspoon salt
1 large egg, at room temperature
1 cup buttermilk or Homemade Buttermilk (page 29), thinned with
   ¼ cup water, well shaken, and at room temperature
¼ cup unsalted butter or buttery spread, at room temperature
½ cup dried currants
1 tablespoon caraway seeds, toasted

1. Place a rack in the middle of the oven. Preheat the oven to 375°F. Generously grease an 8 x 4-inch nonstick (gray, not black) loaf pan.

2. In a large bowl, whisk together the sorghum blend, sugar, baking soda, baking powder, xanthan gum, and salt. Add the egg, buttermilk, butter, currants, and caraway seeds. With an electric mixer on low speed, mix just until thoroughly blended. Spread the batter evenly in the prepared pan and smooth the top with a wet rubber spatula. With a very sharp knife, cut a ⅛-inch-deep X on the top to allow the bread to expand as it rises.

3. Bake until the top is deeply browned and the loaf sounds hollow when tapped, 55 to 60 minutes. The internal temperature should reach 205°F when an instant-read thermometer is inserted into the center of the loaf. Cool in the pan on a wire rack for 10 minutes. Remove the bread from the pan and cool completely on the wire rack. Slice with an electric or serrated knife.

✹ Herb Popovers

MAKES 6 POPOVERS

Popovers are super simple; whip up the batter in a blender and let the oven transform it into bread. If you use dried herbs, crush them in your palm a bit to release their flavor and aroma. Remove the popover's soft interior and stuff with sandwich filling such as chicken salad or tuna salad for a quick lunch.

3 large eggs, at room temperature
I cup milk of choice, at room temperature
⅔ cup potato starch
¼ cup Carol's Sorghum Blend (page 14)
I tablespoon unsalted butter or buttery spread, melted
½ teaspoon salt
¼ teaspoon xanthan gum
I tablespoon finely snipped fresh chives or I teaspoon dried
I tablespoon finely snipped fresh rosemary or I teaspoon dried
2 teaspoons finely chopped fresh sage or ½ teaspoon dried, rubbed

1. Place a rack in the lower-middle position of the oven. Preheat the oven to 450°F. Lightly grease each cup of a standard 6-cup popover pan.

2. In a blender, thoroughly blend all the ingredients, except the herbs. Add the herbs and pulse just a few times to incorporate but not chop them.

3. Place the empty pan in the oven for 5 minutes. Using potholders or oven mitts, carefully remove the hot pan from the oven and fill each cup halfway with batter. Divide the remaining batter evenly among the cups.

4. Bake 20 minutes at 450°F, then reduce the heat to 350°F and continue baking until the sides of the popovers are rigid, about 10 minutes. Do not open the oven door during this time. Quickly— and carefully—remove the pan from the oven. Pierce each popover along the rigid side with a toothpick to release the steam; return the pan to the oven to bake another 5 minutes. Cool in the pan on a wire rack for 5 minutes. Remove the popovers from the pan and serve immediately.

Banana Bread

MAKES 12 SERVINGS

Moist and delicious, this banana bread features nutritious chia seeds (see "What Are Chia Seeds?," page 40),
which add a great crunchy texture to this otherwise soft
and moist bread. You can also use the same amount of
chopped nuts in place of chia seeds. Spread it with peanut butter for a healthy kid's treat.

2 large eggs, at room temperature
¾ cup sugar
1 cup mashed very ripe bananas (about 3 small)
⅓ cup canola oil
1 teaspoon pure vanilla extract
1½ cups Carol's Sorghum Blend (page 14)
1 teaspoon xanthan gum
½ teaspoon salt
2 teaspoons baking powder
1 teaspoon ground cinnamon
½ cup dark raisins
2 tablespoons chia seeds

1. Place a rack in the middle of the oven. Preheat the oven to
350°F. Generously grease 3 mini 5 x 3-inch nonstick (gray, not
black) loaf pans.

2. In a medium bowl, beat the eggs with an electric mixer on
medium speed for 30 seconds. Beat in the sugar until well blended,
then add the banana, oil, and vanilla and beat until smooth.

3. In a separate medium bowl, whisk together the sorghum
blend, xanthan gum, salt, baking powder, and cinnamon. With the
mixer on low speed, gradually beat the flour mixture into the liquid
ingredients until they are well blended and the batter thickens
slightly. Stir in the raisins and chia seeds. Spread evenly in the prepared pan with a wet rubber spatula.

4. Bake until a toothpick inserted into the center of the loaf
comes out clean, 45 to 50 minutes. Cool the bread in the pan on a
wire rack for 10 minutes. Remove the bread from the pans and cool
completely on a wire rack. Slice with an electric or serrated knife.

BANANA BREAD with SALBA

In step 3, use the same amount of salba seeds in place of the chia seeds.

WHAT ARE CHIA SEEDS?

Salvia hispanica, is a member of the mint family and was prized by the Aztecs for its nutritional value. It is increasingly used in gluten-free foods, such as nutrition or energy bars, and can be purchased in natural food stores or online. The chia seeds are related to, but not the same as, the type that sprout on a clay "pet." Like flax and hemp, it provides an important source of fiber and other important nutrients for the gluten-free diet. Its pleasant, nutty flavor makes it a versatile, tasty addition in cookies, muffins, breads, or just sprinkled on yogurt, cereal, or ice cream. It resembles poppy seeds in color and shape.

WHAT IS SALBA?

Like chia, salba is also a member of the mint family, but it has more protein and omega-3s than chia. Prized by the Aztecs for its nutritional value, it contains both soluble and insoluble fiber and is increasingly found in gluten-free foods, such as chips. The seeds are light tan and similar to flax seeds in size and shape. Mild in flavor, the seeds can be added to muffins and bread. Or grind them into a powder and whisk in water to make an egg replacer. Two teaspoons ground salba in ½ cup water makes ¼ cup—enough to replace I large egg. (The seeds absorb 9 times their weight in water and actually reduce down from ½ to ¼ cup in the process.)

Old-Fashioned Molasses Quick Bread

MAKES 12 SERVINGS

This flavorful bread harkens back to the days when molasses, with its distinctive, almost malty flavor, was the sweetener of choice. Serve the bread with savory soups, or spread it with apple or pumpkin butter for a quick breakfast. For added fiber, add ¼ cup of finely chopped nuts or cooked quinoa or teff to the batter.

½ cup milk of choice
1 tablespoon apple cider vinegar or fresh lemon juice
2 cups Carol's Sorghum Blend (page 14)
½ cup gluten-free yellow cornmeal
½ cup potato starch
1½ teaspoons xanthan gum
1 teaspoon salt
1 teaspoon baking soda
2 large eggs, at room temperature
½ cup molasses (not blackstrap)
¼ cup canola oil
1 teaspoon sesame seeds, for sprinkling (optional)

1. Place a rack in the middle of the oven. Preheat the oven to 325°F. Generously grease a 9 × 5-inch nonstick (gray, not black) loaf pan; set aside. In a small measuring cup, whisk together the milk and vinegar and let stand 5 minutes.

2. In a large bowl, whisk together the sorghum blend, cornmeal, potato starch, xanthan gum, salt, and baking soda. Using an electric mixer on low speed, beat in the milk-vinegar mixture, eggs, molasses, and oil until the batter is smooth. Transfer the batter to the prepared pan and smooth the top with a wet rubber spatula. Sprinkle with the sesame seeds, if using.

3. Bake until a toothpick inserted into the center of the loaf comes out clean, 45 to 60 minutes. Cool the bread in the pan on a wire rack for 10 minutes. Remove the bread from the pan and cool for 15 to 20 minutes on the wire rack. Slice with an electric or serrated knife. Serve warm.

✴ Cranberry-Orange Scones with Orange Glaze

MAKES 8 SCONES

Scones are a hearty solution to our cravings for bread. They're perfect for weekend brunches, but also reheat nicely during the week. Serve them with a citrus marmalade.

SCONES
⅓ cup unsalted butter or buttery spread, at room temperature
I tablespoon grated orange zest
I large egg, at room temperature
⅓ cup granulated sugar, plus I tablespoon for sprinkling
½ cup milk of choice
I ½ cups Carol's Sorghum Blend (page 14)
½ cup tapioca flour
I tablespoon baking powder
I ½ teaspoons xanthan gum
I teaspoon guar gum
I teaspoon salt
¾ cup dried cranberries
2 tablespoons heavy cream or milk of choice, for brushing

GLAZE
I to 2 tablespoons fresh orange juice
I cup powdered sugar

1. Place a rack in the middle of the oven. Preheat the oven to 375°F. Generously grease a 13 x 9-inch nonstick (gray, not black) baking sheet or line with parchment paper.

2. Make the scones: In a food processor, process the butter, orange zest, egg, and ⅓ cup sugar until well blended. Add the milk, sorghum blend, tapioca flour, baking powder, xanthan gum, guar gum, and salt, and process just until blended. Add the cranberries and pulse just until the cranberries are incorporated into the dough. The dough will be very soft.

3. Place the dough on the prepared baking sheet, patting it with a wet rubber spatula into a smooth, uniform 8-inch circle about ¾ inch thick. Use the wet spatula to shape straight sides (rather than rounded) for more even browning. Brush the dough with cream and sprinkle with the remaining tablespoon of sugar.

4. Bake until the dough is lightly browned, about 20 minutes. Remove the scones from the oven and, using a sharp knife, cut the circle of dough into 8 wedges. Pull the wedges away from the center so they are at least 1 inch from each other and return the scones to the oven. Bake until the sides of each scone are browned, 5 to 7 minutes more. (This makes all edges of the scones crisp, rather than just the tops.) Cool the scones on the baking sheet on a wire rack for 5 minutes.

5. Make the glaze: In a small bowl, stir the orange juice into the powdered sugar to create a smooth, thin glaze. Using a pastry brush, brush the glaze onto the warm scones. Serve immediately.

BLUEBERRY-LEMON SCONES with LEMON GLAZE

In step 2, replace the cranberries with dried blueberries and the orange zest with lemon zest. In step 5, replace the orange juice with lemon juice.

Chocolate Chip Muffins with White Chocolate Drizzle

MAKES 12 MUFFINS

Serve these dark, dense, and decadent muffins slightly warm so the chips are soft, with a robust coffee.

MUFFINS
- 2 large eggs, at room temperature
- 1 cup milk of choice, warm (about 110°F)
- ½ cup canola oil
- 2 teaspoons pure vanilla extract
- 1½ cups Carol's Sorghum Blend (page 14)
- ¾ cup sugar
- ½ cup Hershey's Special Dark cocoa powder
- 1½ teaspoons xanthan gum
- 1 teaspoon baking soda
- 1 teaspoon salt
- ¾ cup gluten-free semisweet chocolate chips
- ¼ cup slivered almonds

DRIZZLE
- ½ cup chopped gluten-free white chocolate, melted
- 1 to 2 tablespoons milk of choice

1. Place a rack in the middle of the oven. Preheat the oven to 375°F. Generously grease each cup of a standard 12-cup nonstick (gray, not black) muffin pan or line with paper liners.

2. Make the muffins: In a medium bowl, beat the eggs with an electric mixer on low speed for about 30 seconds. Add the milk, oil, and vanilla and beat on low speed just until blended.

3. In a small bowl, whisk together the sorghum blend, sugar, cocoa, xanthan gum, baking soda, and salt. With the mixer on low speed, gradually beat the flour mixture into the liquid ingredients until the batter is smooth and slightly thickened, about 1 to 2 minutes. Stir in the chocolate chips and almonds. Divide the batter evenly in the muffin pan.

4. Bake until the muffin tops are firm, or until a toothpick inserted into the center of a muffin comes out clean, 20 to 25 minutes. Cool the muffins in the pan for 10 minutes. Transfer the muffins to a wire rack to cool another 5 minutes.

5. Make the drizzle: In a small bowl, whisk together the white chocolate and enough milk to make a thin smooth frosting. Drizzle the white chocolate mixture back and forth across the tops of the muffins. Serve immediately.

☺ Basic Muffins with Streusel Topping

MAKES 12 MUFFINS

Muffins are a quick, easy, confidence-inspiring way to incorporate bread into the gluten-free diet because their small size means faster baking than loaf breads. Modify this basic recipe with your favorite add-ins (such as chopped fruit, nuts, or flavorings like almond or rum extracts). Keep a batch in the freezer for the kids' school activities or parties.

STREUSEL TOPPING

½ cup packed light brown sugar
½ cup finely chopped pecans
¼ cup Carol's Sorghum Blend (page 14)
1 teaspoon ground cinnamon
1 teaspoon grated lemon zest
2 tablespoons unsalted butter or buttery spread, melted

MUFFINS

2 large eggs, at room temperature
⅓ cup milk of choice
⅓ cup canola oil
2 teaspoons grated lemon zest
1 teaspoon pure vanilla extract
1¾ cups Carol's Sorghum Blend (page 14)
¾ cup packed light brown sugar
1 tablespoon baking powder
1½ teaspoons xanthan gum
1 teaspoon ground cinnamon
1 teaspoon salt

1. Make the streusel topping: In a small bowl, mix all the streusel ingredients together with a pastry blender until thoroughly blended; set aside.

2. Place a rack in the middle of the oven. Preheat the oven to 375°F. Generously grease each cup of a standard 12-cup nonstick (gray, not black) muffin pan or line with paper liners.

3. Make the muffins: In a medium bowl, beat the eggs with an electric mixer on low speed until light yellow and frothy, about 30 seconds. Add the milk, oil, lemon zest, and vanilla and beat on low speed until the mixture is smooth and slightly thickened, about 1 minute.

☻ Vegetarian ☺ Kids' Favorite ☽ Quick

4. In a small bowl, whisk together the sorghum blend, brown sugar, baking powder, xanthan gum, cinnamon, and salt. With the mixer on low speed, gradually beat the flour mixture into the liquid ingredients until the batter is smooth and slightly thickened. Divide the batter evenly in the pan. Sprinkle 1 tablespoon of streusel topping on each muffin, gently pressing the topping lightly into the batter. (Refrigerate any leftover streusel.)

5. Bake until the muffin tops are firm and the edges start to pull away from the pan, 20 to 25 minutes. Cool the muffins in the pan for 10 minutes. Transfer the muffins to a wire rack to cool another 5 minutes. Serve warm.

FRUIT MUFFINS with STREUSEL TOPPING

In step 4, stir 1 cup fresh raspberries or blueberries into the batter.

😊 White Sandwich Yeast Bread

MAKES ONE ½-POUND LOAF

This is the perfect sandwich bread for families who prefer "white" bread. It is also a good bread to keep on hand
for making French toast for the kids or Plain Bread
Crumbs (see page 49), Italian Bread Crumbs (page 49),
or Croutons (see page 76) that are lighter in color.

1 packet (2¼ teaspoons) active dry yeast
2 tablespoons sugar
1 cup warm water (about 110°F)
White rice flour, for dusting
½ cup egg whites (about 3 large egg whites), at room temperature
2 cups potato starch
1 cup Carol's Sorghum Blend (page 14)
2 teaspoons xanthan gum
1 teaspoon guar gum
1 teaspoon salt
¼ cup unsalted butter or buttery spread, at room temperature,
   or canola oil
2 teaspoons apple cider vinegar
1 teaspoon sesame seeds

1. In a small bowl, dissolve the yeast and 1 teaspoon of the sugar
in the water. Set aside to foam, about 5 minutes.

2. Generously grease a 9 × 5-inch nonstick (gray, not black) loaf
pan. Dust the bottom and sides of the pan lightly with rice flour.

3. In the large bowl of a heavy-duty mixer, beat the egg whites
on medium speed until thick and foamy, about 30 seconds. Add the
potato starch, sorghum blend, xanthan gum, guar gum, salt, butter,
vinegar, remaining sugar, and yeast mixture. Beat on low speed to
gently blend the ingredients, then increase the speed to medium
and beat 30 seconds more or until the mixture is thoroughly combined and slightly thickened.

4. Transfer the dough to the prepared pan and smooth the top
with a wet rubber spatula. Coat the top with cooking spray and
sprinkle with sesame seeds, pressing them gently into the dough
with your fingers. Cover lightly with aluminum foil, and let rise in a
warm place (75°F to 80°F) until the dough is level with the top of
the pan.

5. Place a rack in the middle of the oven. Preheat the oven to 375°F. With a sharp knife, make three diagonal slashes (⅛ inch deep) in the top of the loaf so steam can escape during baking. Bake 1 hour, or until the temperature reaches 205°F on an instant-read thermometer inserted into the center of the loaf. Remove the bread from the oven and cool in the pan on a wire rack for 10 minutes. Remove the bread from the pan and cool completely on the wire rack. Slice with an electric or serrated knife.

PLAIN BREAD CRUMBS

Place 4 cups gluten-free bread of choice, torn into small pieces, in a food processor. Pulse until the crumbs reach the desired consistency. Store tightly covered in the refrigerator for up to 2 weeks and in the freezer up to 3 months.

ITALIAN BREAD CRUMBS

Add 1 teaspoon onion powder and 4 teaspoons Italian herb seasoning to the recipe above; toss well.

✤ High-Fiber Bran Yeast Bread

MAKES ONE 1½-POUND LOAF

High-fiber breads require more yeast and a somewhat longer rising time, but your reward is hearty, nutritious bread that makes great sandwiches or pleasantly chewy toast for breakfast.

    1 tablespoon active dry yeast
    2 tablespoons sugar
    1¾ cups warm milk of choice (about 110°F)
    White rice flour, for dusting
    2 large eggs, at room temperature
    1½ cups potato starch
    ½ cup Carol's Sorghum Blend (page 14)
    ¼ cup rice bran
    2 tablespoons Montina Pure Supplement
    2 tablespoons almond meal or hemp seed
    1 tablespoon apple pectin
    1 teaspoon xanthan gum
    1 teaspoon guar gum
    1 teaspoon salt
    ¼ cup canola oil
    2 teaspoons apple cider vinegar
    2 tablespoons sesame seeds
    1 egg white, beaten until foamy, for egg wash (optional)

1. In a small bowl, dissolve the yeast and 1 teaspoon of the sugar in the milk. Set aside to foam, about 5 minutes.

2. Generously grease a 9 × 5-inch nonstick (gray, not black) loaf pan. Dust the bottom and sides of the pan lightly with rice flour.

3. In the large bowl of a heavy-duty mixer, beat the eggs until light and frothy, about 30 seconds. Add the potato starch, sorghum blend, rice bran, Montina, almond meal, apple pectin, xanthan gum, guar gum, salt, oil, vinegar, remaining sugar, and the yeast-milk mixture. Beat on low speed to blend, then increase the speed to medium and beat 30 seconds or until the mixture is thoroughly combined and slightly thickened. Stir in all but ½ teaspoon of the sesame seeds.

4. Transfer the dough to the prepared pan and smooth the top with a wet rubber spatula. Brush the top with the egg-white wash, if using. Sprinkle the remaining ½ teaspoon of sesame seeds on top, gently pressing into the dough with your fingers. Cover loosely with aluminum foil and let rise in a warm place (75°F to 80°F) until the dough is 1 inch above the top of the pan.

5. Place a rack in the middle of the oven. Preheat the oven to 375°F. With a sharp knife, make three diagonal slashes (⅛ inch deep) in the top of the loaf so steam can escape during baking.

6. Bake until the temperature reaches 205°F on an instant-read thermometer inserted into the center of the loaf, about 1 hour. Remove the bread from the oven and cool in the pan on a wire rack for 10 minutes. Remove the bread from the pan and cool completely on the wire rack. Slice with an electric or serrated knife.

✵ Light Rye Beer Yeast Bread

MAKES ONE 1½-POUND LOAF

Perfect for deli sandwiches, this light rye bread can be made with club soda rather than beer, if you wish, but the flavor will not be as fully developed.

1 tablespoon active dry yeast
¼ cup warm milk of choice (about 110°F)
White rice flour, for dusting
¾ cup gluten-free beer
2 large eggs, at room temperature and lightly beaten
   (reserve 1 tablespoon for egg wash)
2 tablespoons canola oil
2 tablespoons molasses (not blackstrap)
1½ tablespoons packed light brown sugar
1 teaspoon grated orange zest
2 cups Carol's Sorghum Blend (page 14)
1 cup potato starch
2 tablespoons caraway seeds
1 teaspoon instant espresso coffee powder
1 teaspoon salt
1 teaspoon xanthan gum
½ teaspoon onion powder

1. In the large bowl of a heavy-duty stand mixer, dissolve the yeast in the milk. Set aside to foam, about 5 minutes.

2. Generously grease a 9 × 5-inch nonstick (gray, not black) loaf pan. Dust the bottom and sides of the pan lightly with rice flour.

3. Add the beer, eggs, oil, molasses, brown sugar, and orange zest to the yeast mixture and beat on low speed until blended. In a separate large bowl, whisk together the sorghum blend, potato starch, caraway seeds, espresso powder, salt, xanthan gum, and onion powder. With the mixer on low speed, gradually beat the dry ingredients into the wet ingredients until the dough is smooth, about 30 seconds.

4. Transfer the dough to the prepared pan and smooth the top with a wet rubber spatula. Cover loosely with aluminum foil and let rise in a warm place (75°F to 80°F) until the dough is level with the top of the pan.

5. Place a rack in the middle of the oven. Preheat the oven to 375°F. Whisk the reserved 1 tablespoon of egg with 1 tablespoon water until very smooth and brush it on top of the dough. With a sharp knife, make three diagonal slashes (⅛ inch deep) in the top of the loaf so steam can escape during baking. Bake until the tempera-ture reaches 205°F on an instant thermometer inserted into the center of the loaf, about 1 hour. Cover with aluminum foil if the bread starts to brown too quickly.

6. Remove the bread from the oven and cool in the pan on a wire rack for 10 minutes. Remove the bread from the pan and cool completely on the wire rack. Slice with an electric or serrated knife.

Cinnamon Raisin Yeast Bread

MAKES ONE 1½-POUND LOAF

This bread makes great toast, delicious bread pudding, or French toast for the kids. Currants work better than raisins since they're smaller and don't weigh down the dough as much.

1 tablespoon active dry yeast
1 cup warm milk of choice (about 110°F)
¼ cup packed dark brown sugar
White rice flour, for dusting
2 large eggs, at room temperature
1¾ cups potato starch
1 cup Carol's Sorghum Blend (page 14)
2 teaspoons xanthan gum
1 teaspoon salt
¾ teaspoon ground cinnamon
⅓ cup canola oil
2 teaspoons apple cider vinegar
⅔ cup currants or dark raisins tossed with 1 teaspoon potato starch

1. In a small bowl, combine the yeast, milk, and 1 teaspoon of the sugar. Set aside to foam, about 5 minutes. Generously grease a 9 × 5-inch nonstick (gray, not black) loaf pan. Dust the bottom and sides of the pan lightly with rice flour.

2. In the large bowl of a heavy-duty stand mixer, beat the eggs until light and frothy, about 30 seconds. Add the potato starch, sorghum blend, xanthan gum, salt, cinnamon, oil, vinegar, remaining sugar, and yeast mixture and beat on low speed until blended. Increase the speed to medium and beat 30 seconds. Stir in the currants. The dough will be somewhat softer than most yeast breads.

3. Transfer the dough to the prepared pan, smoothing the top with a wet rubber spatula. Cover the dough lightly with aluminum foil and let rise in a warm place (75°F to 80°F) until the dough is level with the top of the pan.

4. Place a rack in the middle of the oven. Preheat the oven to 375°F. With a sharp knife, make three diagonal slashes (⅛ inch deep) in the top of the loaf so steam can escape during baking.

5. Bake until the temperature reaches 205°F on an instant-read thermometer inserted into the center of the loaf, about 1 hour. Do not underbake. Cover with an aluminum foil tent after 20 minutes to reduce overbrowning. Remove from the oven and cool the bread in the pan on a wire rack for 10 minutes. Remove the bread from the pan and cool completely on the wire rack. Slice with an electric or serrated knife.

✺ French Yeast Bread

MAKES 2 FRENCH BREAD LOAVES, ¾ POUND EACH OR 3 FRENCH
BAGUETTE LOAVES, ⅓ POUND EACH

A crispy crust makes this loaf bread a delight to eat. It
makes fantastic bruschetta and crostini. Bake it in a
2-loaf French bread pan for regular French bread, or in
a 3-loaf French baguette pan for baguettes (see step 3).
Notice that the bread starts baking in a cold oven, a very
effective method for this type of bread because it produces a crisper crust and airier texture, and takes less time
to bake because it rises while the oven preheats.

2 tablespoons active dry yeast
2 tablespoons sugar
1 cup plus 2 tablespoons warm water (about 110°F)
½ cup egg whites (about 3 large eggs), at room temperature and
  lightly beaten (reserve 1 tablespoon for egg wash)
2 cups potato starch
1 cup Carol's Sorghum Blend (page 14)
1 teaspoon xanthan gum
1 teaspoon guar gum
1 teaspoon salt
¼ cup unsalted butter or buttery spread, at room temperature,
  or canola oil
2 teaspoons apple cider vinegar
1 teaspoon sesame seeds

1. In a small bowl, dissolve the yeast and 1 teaspoon of the sugar
in warm water. Set aside to foam, about 5 minutes. Generously grease
a French bread pan or line with parchment paper and set aside.

2. In the large bowl of a heavy-duty stand mixer, combine the
egg whites, potato starch, sorghum blend, xanthan gum, guar gum,
salt, butter, vinegar, remaining sugar, and yeast mixture. Beat on low
speed to blend. Beat on medium speed for 30 seconds, stirring down
the sides with a rubber spatula, if necessary. The dough will be soft.

3. Divide the dough in half for French bread or in thirds for
French baguettes and place in the prepared pan. (For equal-size
loaves, use a #12 metal spring-action ice cream scoop to place the
same number of equal-size dough balls in each pan's indentations.)
Shape the dough in each indentation into a 10-inch log with a wet
rubber spatula, taking care to make each loaf the same length and
thickness, with blunt rather than tapered ends. Brush the top of
each loaf with the egg wash for a glossier crust. With a sharp knife,
make three diagonal slashes (⅛ inch deep) in the top of each loaf

(continued on following page)

so steam can escape during baking. Sprinkle with sesame seeds.

4. Place on the middle rack in a cold oven. Set the oven to 425°F and bake until nicely browned, 30 to 35 minutes. Cover the loaves with aluminum foil after 15 minutes of baking to prevent overbrowning.

5. Remove the bread from the pans and cool completely on a wire rack. Slice with an electric knife or serrated knife.

SOURDOUGH FRENCH BREAD

Reduce yeast to 1 tablespoon. In step 2, add ½ cup Sourdough Starter (see below) with the yeast mixture and continue as directed.

SOURDOUGH STARTER

MAKES 3 CUPS

I have always wanted to make a sourdough starter, so I turned to my antique 1940s cookbook, which instructed me to use potato water rather than plain tap water. I use white rice flour in place of the traditional wheat flour because its neutral flavor and white color won't interfere with the flavor or color of my baked goods. Although my nostalgic cookbook doesn't mention it, today we know that it is better to use filtered or bottled spring water because the chlorine in regular tap water interferes with yeast fermentation and may leave a chlorinated aftertaste.

> 1½ cups warm potato water (leftover water from boiling
>   potatoes; about 110°F)
> 1 packet (2¼ teaspoons) active dry yeast
> 1 teaspoon sugar
> 1½ cups white rice flour

1. In a 2-quart glass bowl or crock, combine the potato water, yeast, and sugar and stir until combined. Whisk in the rice flour until the mixture is smooth and about the consistency of pancake batter. Cover loosely with plastic wrap and let sit for 1 to 3 days on your countertop to ferment. It will bubble up at first and you'll need to stir it down.

2. Once the starter is fermented, store it tightly covered in a glass jar or bowl in the refrigerator. Bring it to room temperature right before you are ready to bake and stir it before using. To replenish the starter after you make 1 loaf of bread, whisk in 1 cup lukewarm filtered or bottled water and 1 cup white rice flour until smooth. If you make 2 loaves of bread, replenish the starter with 2 cups water and 2 cups flour. Store tightly covered in the refrigerator.

✸ Pumpernickel French Yeast Bread

MAKES TWO ¾-POUND LOAVES

This French bread style of long, thin loaves makes little slices, but they're convenient and easy to use, especially for sandwiches such as Reubens, or toast them for crostini appetizers.

2 tablespoons active dry yeast
3 tablespoons packed light brown sugar
I cup warm milk of choice (about 110°F)
2 cups Carol's Sorghum Blend (page 14)
I cup cornstarch
2 tablespoons unsweetened cocoa powder
2 tablespoons caraway seeds
I teaspoon onion powder
I teaspoon xanthan gum
I teaspoon guar gum
1½ teaspoons salt
¼ cup canola oil
I tablespoon molasses (not blackstrap)
2 large eggs, at room temperature
I teaspoon grated orange zest
I teaspoon apple cider vinegar
I egg white, beaten, for egg wash

1. In a small bowl, dissolve the yeast and 1 teaspoon of the sugar in the milk. Set aside to foam, about 5 minutes. Generously grease a French bread pan or line with parchment paper.

2. In the large bowl of a heavy-duty stand mixer, combine all the remaining ingredients except for the egg wash. Add the remaining sugar and yeast mixture and beat on low speed just until blended. Then beat on medium speed for 30 seconds, scraping down the sides with a rubber spatula, if necessary. The dough will be soft.

3. Divide the dough in half and place in the prepared pan. Smooth each half into a 10-inch log with a wet rubber spatula. Brush the top of each loaf with the egg wash for a glossier crust. Make three diagonal slashes (⅛ inch deep) in the top of each loaf so steam can escape during baking.

4. Place on the middle rack in a cold oven. Set the oven to 425°F and bake until nicely browned or the temperature reaches 205°F on an instant-read thermometer inserted into the center of the loaf, 30 to 35 minutes.

5. Remove the bread from the pans and cool completely on a wire rack. Slice with an electric or serrated knife.

☺ Pepperoni Pizza
MAKES ONE 12-INCH PIZZA

This light, thin-crusted pizza is one of my most popular recipes ever. Kids love it. The thick pizza sauce is perfect for gluten-free crusts because it doesn't soak into the crust and make it soggy. You can use your own favorite toppings instead of pepperoni, if you wish.

BASIL PIZZA SAUCE
1 (8-ounce) can tomato sauce
2 teaspoons coarsely chopped fresh basil or 1 teaspoon dried
2 teaspoons coarsely chopped fresh flat-leaf parsley or 1 teaspoon dried
¼ teaspoon fennel seeds
¼ teaspoon garlic powder
¼ teaspoon salt
⅛ teaspoon sugar

PIZZA CRUST
1 tablespoon active dry yeast
2½ teaspoons sugar
⅔ cup warm milk of choice (about 110°F)
⅔ cup potato starch
½ cup Carol's Sorghum Blend (page 14)
2 teaspoons xanthan gum
1 teaspoon Italian seasoning
1 teaspoon onion powder
¾ teaspoon salt
2 tablespoons olive oil
2 teaspoons apple cider vinegar
Shortening for greasing pizza pan (do not use cooking spray)
White rice flour, for dusting

TOPPINGS
About 24 gluten-free pepperoni slices, or to taste
1 cup grated mozzarella cheese or cheese alternative

1. Make the sauce: Combine all the sauce ingredients in a small saucepan. Simmer 15 minutes over medium heat and set aside. Makes about 1 cup, enough for one 12-inch pizza.

2. Make the crust: In a small bowl, dissolve the yeast and sugar in the milk. Set aside to foam, about 5 minutes. In a food processor, blend the yeast mixture, potato starch, sorghum blend, xanthan gum, Italian seasoning, onion powder, salt, 1 tablespoon of oil, and vinegar, until a ball forms. The dough will be very soft.

(continued on following page)

3. Place a rack in the bottom position and another in the middle position of the oven. Preheat the oven to 425°F. Generously grease a 12-inch nonstick (gray, not black) pizza pan with shortening. (Do not use cooking spray—it makes it harder to shape the dough.)

4. Place the dough on the prepared pan. Liberally dust the dough with the white rice flour; then press the dough into the pan with your hands, continuing to dust the dough with flour to prevent sticking, as needed. The smoother the dough, the smoother the baked crust will be. Make the edges thicker to contain the toppings. Bake the pizza crust on bottom rack until the crust begins to brown on the bottom, about 15 minutes. Remove the crust from the oven.

5. Brush the crust with the sauce and arrange a single layer of pepperoni slices on top. Sprinkle the mozzarella over the top. Shift the pizza to the middle rack of the oven and bake until the top is nicely browned, 15 to 20 minutes more. Remove the pizza from oven and let stand 5 minutes. Brush the rim of the crust with the remaining 1 tablespoon oil before cutting into 6 slices. Serve immediately.

MARGHERITA PIZZA

In step 5, top the pizza crust with 2 to 3 thinly sliced medium ripe tomatoes, 8 fresh basil leaves, and 1 cup grated mozzarella cheese or cheese alternative. Bake the pizza until the top is nicely browned, 15 to 18 minutes. Brush the rim of the crust with 1 tablespoon olive oil before cutting into 6 slices. Serve immediately.

Soft Pretzels

MAKES 12 PRETZELS

One of my most requested recipes, these soft pretzels can be eaten plain or with lots of mustard or cheese spread, just like the ones you buy in shopping malls.

1 tablespoon active dry yeast
1 tablespoon sugar
⅔ cup warm milk of choice (about 110°F)
½ cup sorghum flour
½ cup potato starch
1 tablespoon buttermilk powder or nonfat dry milk powder (not Carnation), or gluten-free dairy alternative
2 teaspoons xanthan gum
1 teaspoon onion powder
½ teaspoon table salt
1 tablespoon olive oil
2 teaspoons apple cider vinegar
1 large egg white, well beaten, for egg wash
Kosher salt or coarse sea salt
1 tablespoon poppy seeds (optional)

1. In a small bowl, dissolve the yeast and sugar in the milk. Set aside to foam, about 5 minutes. Line a 15 × 10-inch baking sheet (not nonstick) with parchment paper; set aside.

2. In the large bowl of a heavy-duty stand mixer, beat the sorghum flour, potato starch, powdered buttermilk, xanthan gum, onion powder, table salt, oil, vinegar, and yeast mixture on low speed until well blended, about 30 seconds. Increase the speed to high and beat until the dough thickens slightly, about 30 seconds more.

3. Place the dough in a large, heavy-duty food storage bag. Cut ¼ inch from a bottom corner of the bag, making a ⅔-inch circle. Squeeze the dough through the opening onto the prepared baking sheet in the shape of 24 pretzel sticks, each about 3 inches long. It works best to hold the bag upright as you squeeze the dough onto the baking sheet. Brush the pretzels lightly with the beaten egg white, then sprinkle with kosher salt to taste. Let the pretzels rise 20 to 25 minutes in a warm place (80°F to 90°F).

4. Place the baking sheet on the middle rack of a cold oven and set the oven to 400°F. Bake until the pretzels are dry and golden brown, approximately 15 minutes. Remove from the oven and spray lightly with cooking spray. Sprinkle with poppy seeds, if using. Cool the pretzels on the sheet on a wire rack for 15 minutes. Remove the pretzels from the sheet and cool completely on the wire rack.

✳ Focaccia with Herbs

MAKES 10 SERVINGS

Focaccia is a cross between flatbread and pizza; in fact, it is sometimes used as the base for pizza. Serve focaccia as an accompaniment for dinner or as a sandwich bread (sliced horizontally). Leftovers can be made into Croutons (see page 76) or Plain Bread Crumbs (see page 49).

1½ teaspoons active dry yeast
2 teaspoons sugar
½ cup warm water (about 110°F)
White rice flour, for dusting
1½ cups Carol's Sorghum Blend (page 14)
1½ teaspoons xanthan gum
4 teaspoons coarsely snipped fresh rosemary or 2 teaspoon dried, crushed, divided
½ teaspoon onion powder
½ teaspoon table salt
2 large eggs, at room temperature
2 tablespoons extra-virgin olive oil, plus more for brushing
1 teaspoon apple cider vinegar
Olive oil cooking spray
½ teaspoon Italian seasoning
1 teaspoon kosher or coarse sea salt, or to taste

1. In a small bowl, dissolve the yeast and sugar in the water. Set aside to foam, about 5 minutes.

2. Generously grease an 11 × 7-inch nonstick (gray, not black) baking dish. Dust the bottom and sides of the dish lightly with rice flour.

3. In the large bowl of a heavy-duty stand mixer, combine the sorghum blend, xanthan gum, 2 teaspoons rosemary, onion powder, table salt, eggs, oil, vinegar, and yeast mixture. Beat the dough on low speed until thoroughly blended. Increase the speed to medium and continue beating for 30 seconds or until the dough starts to thicken slightly. The dough will be soft and sticky.

4. Transfer the dough to the prepared dish. Spread the dough to the edges of the pan with a wet rubber spatula, making sure the dough is uniformly thick

5. Let the dough rise in a warm place (75°F to 80°F) until the dough is level with the top of the pan. Spray the dough lightly with cooking spray. Sprinkle the dough with the remaining 2 teaspoons rosemary, Italian seasoning, and kosher salt.

(continued on following page)

6. Place a rack in the lower-middle position of the oven. Preheat the oven to 400°F.

7. Bake until the top is golden brown and firm and the temperature reaches 205°F on an instant-read thermometer inserted into the center of the loaf, about 25 minutes. Remove the focaccia from the oven, and cool the focaccia in the pan on a wire rack for 10 minutes. Remove the focaccia from pan and cool on the wire rack for 10 more minutes. Brush lightly with oil. Slice with an electric or serrated knife and serve slightly warm.

✦ Fresh Chive Flatbread with Dipping Oil
MAKES 10 SERVINGS

Enjoy fresh bread, hot from the oven, in 30 minutes with this quick, easy recipe. Quite thin, it is easily torn into bite-size pieces for dipping in the oil.

BREAD
- 1½ teaspoons active dry yeast
- 2 teaspoons sugar
- ¾ cup warm milk of choice (about 110°F)
- 1½ cups Carol's Sorghum Blend (page 14)
- ¼ cup sweet rice flour
- 1 teaspoon xanthan gum
- 2 teaspoons finely snipped fresh rosemary or 1 teaspoon dried, crushed
- ¾ teaspoon table salt
- ½ teaspoon onion powder
- 2 large eggs, at room temperature
- 3 tablespoons olive oil
- 2 teaspoons cider vinegar
- 1 tablespoon Parmesan cheese or cheese alternative, for garnish
- 1 tablespoon coarsely chopped fresh chives
- 1 teaspoon kosher or coarse sea salt, or to taste

DIPPING OIL
- ¼ cup extra-virgin olive oil
- Coarse salt and freshly ground black pepper to taste
- 2 tablespoons balsamic vinegar
- ½ teaspoon dried oregano
- ½ teaspoon dried thyme

1. Make the bread: In a small bowl, dissolve the yeast and sugar in the milk. Set aside to foam, about 5 minutes. Generously grease a 13 x 9-inch nonstick (gray, not black) pan or baking sheet.

2. In a large bowl, whisk together the sorghum blend, rice flour, xanthan gum, rosemary, table salt, and onion powder . Add the yeast mixture, eggs, 2 tablespoons oil, and vinegar and beat with an electric mixer on low speed until the dough thickens, about 1 minute. The dough will be soft and very sticky.

3. Transfer the dough to the prepared baking sheet and smooth the top with a wet rubber spatula into a thin layer out to the edges of the pan. Sprinkle with the remaining 1 tablespoon oil, the Parmesan, chives, and kosher salt.

4. Place the pan on the middle rack in a cold oven. Turn the oven to 400°F. Bake until the top is golden brown and firm, 20 to 25 minutes. Remove the bread from the oven and cool slightly in the pan.

5. Make the dipping oil: In a small bowl, whisk together the oil, salt and pepper, vinegar, oregano, and thyme. Place a little dipping oil on each serving plate and serve it with the warm bread, which can be cut or torn into pieces.

Breadsticks

Soft, chewy breadsticks are perfect with an Italian meal, and gluten-free guests are delighted to have something they so rarely get to eat. Breadsticks are also the perfect size for kids because they're smaller and lots more fun to eat than a slice of bread.

1 tablespoon active dry yeast
¾ cup warm milk of choice (about 110°F)
½ cup Carol's Sorghum Blend (page 14)
½ cup potato starch
1 tablespoon sugar
2 teaspoons xanthan gum
½ to ¾ teaspoon salt
2 tablespoons grated Parmesan cheese, Romano cheese, or cheese alternative
1 teaspoon onion powder
1 tablespoon olive oil
2 teaspoons apple cider vinegar
1 egg white, well beaten, for egg wash
1 teaspoon sesame seeds (optional)

1. In a small bowl, dissolve the yeast in the milk. Set aside to foam, about 5 minutes.

2. Place a rack in the middle of the oven. Generously grease a 15 x 10-inch baking sheet or line with parchment paper.

3. In a food precessor, blend the yeast mixture, sorghum blend, potato starch, sugar, xanthan gum, salt, Parmesan, onion powder, oil, and vinegar until just blended.

4. Place the dough in a large, heavy-duty food storage bag. Cut a ½-inch opening diagonally on a bottom corner, making a 1-inch circle. Squeeze the dough out of the plastic bag and onto the prepared baking sheet in 10 strips, about 1 x 6 inches long. For best results, hold the bag of dough upright as you squeeze, rather than at an angle. Also, hold the bag with the corners perpendicular to the baking sheet, rather than horizontal, for a more authentic-looking breadstick. Brush the breadsticks with the egg white (or coat with cooking spray for a crispier, shinier breadstick). Sprinkle with sesame seeds, if using.

5. Put the baking sheet in the cold oven and turn the oven to 400°F. Bake until the breadsticks are golden brown, 15 to 20 minutes. Rotate the baking sheet a quarter turn halfway through baking to assure even browning. Cool the breadsticks on the baking sheet for 15 minutes. Remove the breadsticks from the sheet to a wire rack and cool 5 minutes more. Serve warm.

SOUPS, SALADS, AND SNACKS

SOUPS
French Onion Soup
Beer Cheese Soup
Chicken Noodle Soup with Dumplings

SALADS
Beet-Orange Salad with Crispy Goat Cheese Rounds
Caesar Salad with Croutons

SNACKS
Olive Puffs
Roasted Artichoke Dip
Crab Cakes
Ham and Cheese Panini
Simple Cheese Quesadillas

French Onion Soup

MAKES 4 SERVINGS

Plan ahead to make this delicious soup because the
onions need to cook for over an hour to reach the deep-
brown caramelizing that produces the soup's extraordi-
nary, full-bodied flavor.

¼ **cup olive oil**
1 **tablespoon unsalted butter or buttery spread**
6 **yellow onions, thinly sliced**
½ **teaspoon salt**
½ **teaspoon freshly ground black pepper**
2 **garlic cloves, minced**
3 **cups gluten-free, low-sodium beef broth**
3 **cups gluten-free, low-sodium chicken broth**
¼ **cup dry white wine, sherry, or vermouth**
1 **tablespoon brandy**
1 **teaspoon sugar**
2 **teaspoons fresh thyme or ½ teaspoon dried**
1 **bay leaf**
1 **tablespoon cornstarch**
4 **(½-inch-thick) slices French Yeast Bread (page 55) or other
   gluten-free French bread**
2 **cups grated Gruyère or cheese alternative**
2 **tablespoons grated Parmesan cheese or cheese alternative, for garnish**

1. In a Dutch oven or other deep, heavy pot with a tight-fitting
lid, heat the oil and butter over medium heat. Add the onions, salt,
and pepper. Cook, stirring occasionally, until the onions soften,
about 10 minutes. Reduce the heat to low and cook slowly, stirring
occasionally, until the onions are caramelized, about 1 hour 15
minutes. (After 30 minutes of cooking, the onions should be light
golden brown; by 45 minutes, the onions will be deep brown.)

2. After the onions have cooked, slowly stir in the garlic, beef
broth, chicken broth, wine, brandy, sugar, thyme, and bay leaf.
Simmer, partially covered, over low heat for 15 minutes. Mix the
cornstarch with 1 tablespoon water, add to the soup, and stir until
thickened.

3. Place a rack in the middle of the oven. Preheat the oven to
325°F. Place the bread slices on a 13 × 9-inch baking sheet (not
nonstick). Bake until dry, 5 minutes per side. (You can do this
ahead of time if you wish.)

4. Preheat the broiler. Remove the bay leaf and discard. Ladle the soup into 4 heatproof soup bowls. Place the bowls in a 13 × 9 × 2-inch baking dish. Place a slice of toasted bread on top of each bowl of soup. Divide the Gruyère equally among the 4 bowls. Broil until golden brown, about 2 to 3 minutes. Serve hot, garnished with the Parmesan.

ALCOHOLIC BEVERAGES

Why is regular beer off-limits for the gluten-free diet, yet most distilled alcoholic beverages are not? Beer is fermented, not distilled, so the gluten from wheat or barley (the most common grains for making beer) remains in the beer. Today, many manufacturers use sorghum instead of wheat and barley to make gluten-free beer. If you can't find gluten-free beer, you may use hard cider (see page 16), which is typically fermented from apples, pears, and sometimes quinces and is gluten-free. In contrast to fermentation, gluten cannot carry over during the distillation process, so scientists assure us that alcoholic beverages distilled from wheat or wheat-related grains, such as scotch or whiskey, are safe for the gluten-free diet. What about wine? It is made from grapes and is gluten-free—unless it is combined with other ingredients that are not, such as barley malt in wine coolers.

Beer Cheese Soup

MAKES 4 SERVINGS

With gluten-free beer (or hard cider) available, now we all can enjoy this soup that is so popular in restaurants and pubs. The rich, creamy cheese blends tantalizingly with the yeasty, sharp flavor of beer. Mild Cheddar melts better than sharp Cheddar.

2 tablespoons unsalted butter or buttery spread
½ cup finely diced onion
½ cup finely diced celery
½ cup finely diced carrot
½ teaspoon salt, or to taste
⅛ teaspoon ground nutmeg
⅛ teaspoon ground cloves
⅙ teaspoon white pepper
2 cups gluten-free, low-sodium chicken broth
2 tablespoons sweet rice flour
2 cups grated mild Cheddar cheese or cheese alternative
1 (12-ounce) bottle gluten-free beer
2 teaspoons coarsely chopped fresh flat-leaf parsley or 1 teaspoon
   dried, for garnish
Sweet paprika, for garnish

1. In a heavy soup pot, heat the butter over medium heat. Add the onion, celery, and carrot and cook, stirring, for 1 minute. Reduce the heat to medium-low, cover, and cook until the onion is soft and translucent, about 5 minutes. Add the salt, nutmeg, cloves, pepper, and 1¾ cups of the broth. Simmer, covered, for 30 minutes.

2. In a medium bowl, whisk the rice flour with the remaining ¼ cup broth until smooth and then add to the soup pot, stirring constantly, until the soup thickens slightly. Remove the soup from the heat and stir in the Cheddar until it is thoroughly melted. Puree the soup in batches in a blender if you prefer a smoother texture.

3. Just before serving, add the beer to the soup and return the soup to the stove, bringing to serving temperature over low heat. Garnish with the parsley and paprika and serve hot.

☺ Chicken Noodle Soup with Dumplings

MAKES 4 SERVINGS

Chicken noodle soup, brimming with dense, hearty dumplings, is the all-American comfort food. It works better to boil the dumplings in a separate pot of broth or water rather than to boil them with the pasta because the pasta will cook faster than the dumplings. Leave the lid on while they are boiling and don't peek until the cooking time is done so the dumplings keep their shape.

DUMPLINGS

- 1½ teaspoons salt
- 1¼ cups Carol's Sorghum Blend (page 14)
- ⅔ cup potato starch
- 2 teaspoons baking powder
- ½ teaspoon baking soda
- 1 large egg
- ¼ cup unsalted butter or buttery spread, at room temperature
- ½ cup buttermilk or Homemade Buttermilk (page 29), well shaken
- 2 tablespoons coarsely chopped flat-leaf fresh parsley

SOUP

- 1 teaspoon canola oil
- ½ cup thinly sliced celery
- ½ cup coarsely chopped onion
- 6 cups gluten-free, low-sodium chicken broth
- 1 small carrot, thinly sliced
- ½ teaspoon poultry seasoning
- ¼ teaspoon salt, or to taste
- ¼ teaspoon white pepper
- ⅛ teaspoon freshly grated nutmeg
- 1 bay leaf
- 1 cup gluten-free pasta of choice
- 1½ cups diced cooked chicken
- 1 tablespoon fresh lemon juice
- ¼ cup coarsely chopped fresh flat-leaf parsley or 2 tablespoons dried, for garnish

1. Make the dumplings: Fill a large soup pot with 4 inches of water and 1 teaspoon salt. Bring to a boil over high heat. Meanwhile, in a medium bowl, whisk together the sorghum blend, potato starch, baking powder, baking soda, and remaining ½ teaspoon salt.

2. In a small bowl, mix together the egg and butter. Gradually mix the egg mixture into the dry ingredients, alternating with the buttermilk, and mix until just moistened. Stir in the parsley. The dough should be stiff.

3. Drop the dough by tablespoonfuls into the boiling water. (Or use a small spring-action metal scoop to drop balls of dough into the water.) Cover, reduce the heat to low, and cook, without lifting the lid, for 20 minutes.

4. Make the soup: In a large, heavy saucepan, heat the oil over medium heat. Add the celery and onion and cook until softened and lightly browned, 3 to 4 minutes. Add the broth, carrot, poultry seasoning, salt, pepper, nutmeg, and bay leaf. Bring to a boil, then reduce the heat to low and cook, covered, 10 to 15 minutes.

5. Add the pasta and chicken and simmer, uncovered, until the chicken is heated through and the pasta is done (cooking times will vary by brand).

6. Stir in the lemon juice at the last minute; remove the bay leaf and discard. Ladle the soup into 4 bowls, remove the dumplings from the water with a slotted spoon, and divide evenly among the 4 bowls. Serve, garnished with the parsley.

✺ Beet-Orange Salad with Crispy Goat Cheese Rounds

MAKES 4 SERVINGS

Serve this lovely beet salad to guests and let its gorgeous ruby, orange, and green colors adorn the table.

SALAD
¼ cup Plain Bread Crumbs (page 49) or other gluten-free bread crumbs
Salt and freshly ground black pepper
1 large egg
4 rounds fresh goat cheese, about 2 ounces each, chilled
1 head butter lettuce, leaves separated.
1 (16-ounce) can sliced red beets, drained
3 navel oranges, peeled and sliced crosswise into rounds
1 small shallot, minced
1 tablespoon coarsely chopped fresh cilantro
2 tablespoons olive oil

CITRUS VINAIGRETTE
3 tablespoons fresh orange juice
1 tablespoon fresh lemon juice
1 teaspoon grated orange zest
1 teaspoon grated lemon zest
1 teaspoon dry mustard
1 tablespoon extra-virgin olive oil
⅛ teaspoon xanthan gum

1. Make the salad: In a small, shallow bowl, mix the bread crumbs with the salt and pepper to taste. In a separate small, shallow bowl, beat the egg just until blended. Dip each cheese round in the egg, and then in the bread crumbs, patting the crumbs in place. Cover and refrigerate for about 15 minutes.

2. Arrange the lettuce leaves on a large platter or 4 individual salad plates. Arrange the beets, oranges, and shallot in the bowls formed by the lettuce. Sprinkle with the cilantro.

3. Heat the oil in a large nonstick skillet over medium-high heat. Add the cheese rounds and fry until lightly browned, about 45 seconds. Turn them over and cook on the other side until the cheese just feels quivery, about 45 seconds longer. Arrange the cheese rounds on the salad.

4. Make the vinaigrette: In a blender, process all the ingredients together until slightly thickened, then drizzle on the salad and serve immediately.

✲ Caesar Salad with Croutons

MAKES 4 SERVINGS

It's the crispy croutons that make Caesar salad off-limits in restaurants, but it's so easy to make at home. And there are no raw eggs to worry about because this delicious version is egg-free.

CROUTONS

- 2 garlic cloves, minced
- ½ teaspoon salt
- ¼ cup extra-virgin olive oil
- 1½ cups gluten-free bread cubes, made from White Sandwich Yeast Bread (page 48) or other gluten-free white bread, crusts removed, and cut in ½-inch cubes

SALAD

- 1 tablespoon fresh lemon juice
- 1 teaspoon apple cider vinegar
- 1 teaspoon dry mustard
- 1 teaspoon gluten-free Worcestershire sauce
- 1 teaspoon anchovy paste (optional)
- 1 head romaine lettuce, torn into bite-size pieces
- ⅓ cup grated Parmesan cheese or cheese alternative

1. Place a rack in the middle of the oven. Preheat the oven to 350°F. Line a 13 × 9-inch baking sheet (not nonstick) with aluminum foil; set aside.

2. In a small bowl, mash the garlic with the salt and oil; set aside.

3. Make the croutons: Place the bread cubes in a single layer on the prepared baking sheet. Bake until they are just lightly browned, about 10 minutes. Transfer the bread cubes to a large bowl, toss them with half of the garlic-oil mixture, and return to the baking sheet. Bake until golden brown and crisp, about 3 to 5 minutes more. Remove from the oven and set aside to cool slightly.

4. Make the salad: In a large salad bowl, whisk together the remaining garlic-oil mixture from the croutons, the lemon juice, vinegar, mustard, Worcestershire sauce, and anchovy paste, if using. Add the lettuce and toss thoroughly. Sprinkle with the Parmesan and add the croutons. Toss again and serve immediately.

✸ Olive Puffs
MAKES 24 PUFFS

No one ever expects to find a whole olive inside these little morsels—but what a pleasant (and delicious) surprise! If you need to bake them right away, freeze for 15 minutes and then bake. You can also freeze the unbaked puffs and bake them up quickly for unexpected guests.

½ cup Carol's Sorghum Blend (page 14)
2 teaspoons coarsely chopped fresh flat-leaf parsley or 1 teaspoon dried
½ teaspoon sweet paprika
⅛ teaspoon onion powder
⅛ teaspoon baking soda
⅛ teaspoon cayenne pepper
1 cup shredded sharp Cheddar cheese or cheese alternative
¼ cup (½ stick) unsalted butter or buttery spread, at room temperature
24 pimiento-stuffed green olives, patted dry

1. In a food processor, combine the sorghum blend, parsley, paprika, onion powder, baking soda, and cayenne. Pulse a few times to blend. Add the Cheddar and butter and pulse until the mixture forms a ball. Remove the dough from the food processor.

2. Shape 1 teaspoon of dough around each olive and place on a plate. Cover and chill for 2 hours or overnight.

3. Place a rack in the middle of the oven. Preheat the oven to 400°F. Generously grease a 13 × 9-inch baking sheet or line with parchment paper. Place the chilled balls on the prepared sheet. Bake until lightly browned, 12 to 15 minutes. Serve immediately.

✵ Roasted Artichoke Dip

MAKES 8 SERVINGS

Keep a package of frozen artichokes in your freezer for this simple, tasty alternative to typical dairy-based dips. Serve with crudités, your favorite crackers, or on toasted French bread.

½ cup fresh lemon juice
⅔ cup extra-virgin olive oil
2 large garlic cloves, minced
½ teaspoon salt
¼ teaspoon freshly ground black pepper
1 (14-ounce) package frozen artichokes, thawed
2 teaspoons dried thyme
2 teaspoons dried basil
2 tablespoons grated Parmesan cheese or cheese alternative

1. Place a rack in the middle of the oven. Preheat the oven to 350°F. In a large, heavy, ovenproof skillet, combine 6 tablespoons lemon juice, 2 tablespoons oil, the garlic, salt, and pepper. Add the artichokes and toss to coat. Bring the mixture to a boil over high heat. Remove from the heat and place the skillet, uncovered, in the oven.

2. Bake until the artichokes are tender and lightly browned, about 30 to 45 minutes. Remove from the oven and cool for 10 minutes.

3. Place the roasted artichokes in a food processor and add the remaining 2 tablespoons lemon juice, the remaining oil, and the thyme, basil, and Parmesan. Process until thoroughly blended. Taste and add additional salt and pepper, if desired. Serve immediately.

QUICK ANTIPASTO TRAY

Keep the fixings on hand for this visually appealing antipasto tray and you could be serving unexpected guests or a quick meal in five minutes. Place a bowl of store-bought hummus in the center of the platter and arrange Boston, butter, or red leaf lettuce leaves around it. In the lettuce leaf hollows, arrange piles of kalamata olives, green olives, pickled hot peppers, such as pepperoncini, roasted red peppers, balls of mozzarella cheese or cubes of your favorite cheese, and gluten-free deli meats such as pepperoni slices. Serve with baskets of gluten-free crackers or breadsticks.

Crab Cakes

MAKES 16 CRAB CAKES

Seafood lovers will adore these crab cakes, laden with mouthwatering lumps of pure crab, without the usual wheat bread crumbs. Serve them with your favorite red cocktail sauce, such as Heinz, or tartar sauce. Or shape them into 8 larger cakes for a main dish.

2 tablespoons mayonnaise
1 tablespoon dried minced onion or ¼ cup finely chopped fresh
2 tablespoons coarsely chopped fresh flat-leaf parsley or 1 tablespoon dried
1 tablespoon Dijon mustard
2 teaspoons Old Bay Seasoning
1 large egg
1 tablespoon gluten-free Worcestershire sauce
1 tablespoon fresh lemon juice
½ teaspoon salt
¼ teaspoon cayenne pepper
1 pound lump crabmeat, picked over for shells and cartilage
1 cup Plain Bread Crumbs (page 49) or other gluten-free bread crumbs
2 tablespoons canola oil, for frying

1. Place a rack in the middle of the oven. Preheat the oven to 300°F. In a large bowl, combine the mayonnaise, onion, parsley, mustard, Old Bay Seasoning, egg, Worcestershire sauce, lemon juice, salt, and cayenne. Gently fold in the crabmeat and bread crumbs.

2. Shape the mixture into 16 cakes, about 1 inch thick. (The crab cakes can be refrigerated overnight at this point, if needed.)

3. In a large, heavy, ovenproof skillet, heat the oil over medium-high heat. Add the crab cakes and cook over medium heat until golden and crisp, 2 to 3 minutes per side. Transfer the skillet to the oven to keep the crab cakes warm until serving time.

SOUTHWESTERN CRAB CAKES

In step 1, replace the Old Bay Seasoning with 2 teaspoons Spice Islands Smoky Mesquite Seasoning and replace the lemon juice with lime juice. Stir in 1 (4-ounce) can drained chopped green chiles with the crab and bread crumbs.

PANINI: SANDWICHES WITH ITALIAN FLAIR

For best results, use thin fillings such as thinly sliced gluten-free deli meat rather than thick chunks of meat. Thick, chunky sauces work better than watery ones. Always include an ingredient that is fairly spicy such as mustard or salsa, very flavorful such as pesto, garlic mayonnaise, or guacamole, or a bit sweet, such as marmalade or jam, to provide pleasing contrast with the crispy bread and savory meat. Panini do not have to contain meat. They can simply be cheese and bread, like a crispy grilled cheese sandwich. Panini can be made ahead, wrapped, and transported to work for reheating in a microwave. You'll lose some of the crispy exterior, but they'll still taste great.

Ham and Cheese Panini

MAKES 4 PANINI

A panino (singular for panini) is an Italian sandwich cooked in a special panini machine—a hinged grill pan with ridges—that presses the sandwich while the ingredients meld and fuse together, much like a compressed grilled cheese sandwich with ridges. Or cook the sandwiches in a heavy skillet, pressed down with another heavy skillet or a foil-covered brick.

8 slices White Sandwich Yeast Bread (page 48) or other gluten-free sandwich bread
4 thin slices Black Forest ham or prosciutto
4 thin slices Swiss cheese, Gruyère, or cheese alternative
4 tablespoons apricot preserves

1. Lay the slices of bread on a flat work surface and lightly coat with cooking spray. Turn 4 of the slices over and layer each with ham and cheese. Spread a tablespoon of preserves on top. Top with the remaining 4 slices of bread, sprayed-side up.

2. Heat a panini press and grill the sandwiches, following the manufacturer's directions. (If you use a skillet, lightly coat the skillet with cooking spray and brown the sandwiches, turning once, and using a heavy object to weigh it down.) Serve immediately.

TURKEY, BRIE, AND APPLE PANINI

For each sandwich, replace the ham with thinly sliced deli turkey and use 1 tablespoon Brie, 1 tablespoon Dijon mustard, and 2 very thin slices of green apple. Cook as directed in step 2.

Simple Cheese Quesadillas

MAKES 2 LARGE QUESADILLAS

Queso means "cheese" in Spanish; quesadillas are toasted Mexican cheese sandwiches made from tortillas instead of bread. Kids love them for dinner or snacks. Feel free to add your favorite fillings in addition to the cheese: shredded chicken, beef, or pork; caramelized onions; black olives; or avocado.

½ **pound shredded Cheddar cheese or cheese alternative**
¼ **cup coarsely chopped fresh cilantro**
I tablespoon canola oil
4 (8- or 9-inch) gluten-free tortilla wraps

1. In a small bowl, combine the Cheddar and cilantro. Set aside.

2. Brush a flat, nonstick (gray, not black) grill pan or skillet large enough to hold the tortillas with half of the oil. Gently lay a tortilla directly on the grill pan. Do not turn on the heat yet.

3. Spoon the cheese mixture over the tortilla. With a spatula, gently spread the filling evenly over the tortilla to within ½ inch of the edge. Lay a second tortilla on top and gently press down.

4. Turn the heat to medium and cook, covered, until the tortillas are gently browned, about 2 to 3 minutes. With a very large spatula or two smaller ones, gently turn the quesadilla. Cook 2 to 3 minutes more. Gently place a cooked tortilla on a flat surface, such as a large cutting board, and cut into quarters with a very sharp knife. Remove the grill pan from the heat to cool slightly before cooking the remaining quesadilla.

5. Repeat with the remaining ingredients. Serve immediately.

REFRIED BEAN QUESADILLAS

Spread ½ cup of refried beans on each set of tortillas, then sprinkle with ¼ cup finely chopped green onion and 2 tablespoons coarsely chopped fresh cilantro before cooking.

GRAINS, BEANS, AND PASTA

GRAINS
Orange-Scented Wild Rice with Dried Fruits
Grilled Vegetables on Brown Rice
Quinoa Tabbouleh
Teff-Corn Polenta

BEANS
Warm Lentils with Herbs
Black-Eyed Peas with Collard Greens and Rice

PASTA
Linguine with White Clam Sauce
Fettuccine Alfredo
Macaroni and Cheese
Spaghetti with Marinara Sauce
Penne Pasta Primavera
Ravioli in Creamy Marinara Sauce
Potato Gnocchi

✪ Orange-Scented Wild Rice with Dried Fruits

MAKES 4 SERVINGS

Wild rice is actually a seed, usually grown in the northern United States. The texture of nutty, crunchy wild rice and the sweet-tart flavor of dried fruit make this an irresistible dish. It especially complements roast pork or roast chicken.

3 cups gluten-free, low-sodium chicken broth
I cup wild rice, rinsed
½ cup finely sliced green onions
½ cup diced dried apricots
½ cup golden raisins
2 tablespoons coarsely chopped fresh flat-leaf parsley
¼ cup pine nuts, toasted
I teaspoon extra-virgin olive oil
2 tablespoons balsamic vinegar or Champagne vinegar
2 tablespoons fresh orange juice
I tablespoon grated orange zest
I small garlic clove, minced
¼ teaspoon salt
⅛ teaspoon freshly ground black pepper

1. In a large pot, bring the broth to a boil over high heat. Add the wild rice, lower the heat, and cook, covered, until tender, about 45 minutes. Drain.

2. In a large ovenproof serving dish, combine the cooked rice with the green onions, apricots, raisins, parsley, and pine nuts. Toss gently.

3. In a glass jar with a lid, combine the oil, vinegar, orange juice and zest, garlic, salt, and pepper. Shake vigorously to blend well. Pour over the rice mixture and toss gently. Serve immediately, or chill for 2 hours for a cold salad.

Grilled Vegetables on Brown Rice

MAKES 6 SERVINGS

Grilling accentuates the flavor of vegetables and the bold marinade infuses even more flavor. If grilling isn't possible, roast the vegetables in the oven.

2 tablespoons extra-virgin olive oil
⅓ cup Champagne vinegar or sherry vinegar
1 teaspoon coarsely chopped fresh oregano leaves or ½ teaspoon dried
2 large garlic cloves, minced
½ teaspoon ground coriander
½ teaspoon smoked paprika
¼ teaspoon ground cumin
¼ teaspoon salt
¼ teaspoon freshly ground black pepper
2 tablespoons molasses (not blackstrap)
1 large yellow onion, quartered
4 large carrots, halved lengthwise
1 large red bell pepper, quartered
1 large yellow bell pepper, quartered
4 small red new potatoes, scrubbed and halved
2 medium zucchini, halved
2 small yellow squash, halved
2 cups hot cooked brown rice

1. In a large bowl, combine the oil, vinegar, oregano, garlic, coriander, paprika, cumin, salt, black pepper, and molasses. Add the onion, carrots, both bell peppers, potatoes, zucchini, and squash and marinate 30 to 45 minutes. Stir occasionally to make sure the vegetables are coated with the marinade.

2. Drain the vegetables, reserving the marinade, and arrange in a grill basket that has been liberally coated with cooking spray. (Withhold the red and yellow bell peppers, zucchini, and squash until the final 10 minutes of grilling so they don't overcook.)

3. Place a barbecue grill about 5 to 6 inches away from the heat source. Preheat the grill. Cook the vegetables on the grill over medium heat with the lid down until done, turning every 5 minutes, about 15 to 20 minutes. The type and thickness of the vegetables determines the cooking time. Add the remaining vegetables during the last 10 minutes.

4. Meanwhile, in a small saucepan, warm the marinade over medium-low heat. Remove the vegetables from the grill basket and toss with the warmed marinade. Serve warm over the rice.

✳ Quinoa Tabbouleh

MAKES 4 SERVINGS

Quinoa, once used by the Aztecs and known as the "mother grain" because of its superior nutrition, is actually a seed related to spinach or beets. You may use the same amount of cooked brown rice or whole sorghum in place of the quinoa. See Cooked Whole Grains for Breakfast (page 23), for cooking times.

QUINOA
- I teaspoon canola oil
- I cup quinoa, rinsed
- 1¾ cups gluten-free, low-sodium chicken broth
- ¾ cup water
- ½ teaspoon salt

TABBOULEH
- ¼ cup shelled raw pumpkin seeds
- I English (hothouse) cucumber, unpeeled and coarsely chopped
- 3 green onions, thinly sliced
- 12 cherry tomatoes, quartered, or 24 grape tomatoes, halved
- ½ cup coarsely chopped flat-leaf fresh parsley
- ½ cup coarsely chopped fresh cilantro
- ¼ cup coarsely chopped fresh mint

DRESSING
- 3 tablespoons fresh lemon juice
- 2 tablespoons extra-virgin olive oil
- I tablespoon white wine vinegar or rice vinegar
- ¼ teaspoon salt
- ⅛ teaspoon white pepper
- ¼ cup crumbled feta cheese (optional)

1. Make the quinoa: In a medium saucepan, heat the oil over medium heat. Add the quinoa, broth, water, and salt, reduce the heat to low, and cook, covered, until the quinoa is tender, about 15 to 20 minutes. Remove from the heat and cool 10 minutes. Drain the quinoa well.

2. Make the tabbouleh: In a large serving bowl, combine the cooked quinoa with the pumpkin seeds, cucumber, green onions, tomatoes, parsley, cilantro, and mint.

3. Make the dressing: In a screw-top jar, combine the lemon juice, oil, vinegar, salt, and pepper and shake vigorously to blend. Pour over the quinoa mixture and toss until thoroughly coated. Cover and refrigerate for 4 hours. Let stand at room temperature 20 minutes before serving. Toss with the feta cheese, if using, just before serving.

✣ Teff-Corn Polenta

MAKES 4 SERVINGS

Teff, a tiny Ethiopian grain filled with valuable nutrients, has a unique texture similar to corn polenta when
cooked. I blend it with traditional polenta for a nuttier
flavor in this innovative dish. Use ivory teff for a lighter
colored polenta.

4 cups gluten-free, low-sodium chicken broth
I teaspoon salt
¾ cup gluten-free yellow cornmeal
¼ cup whole grain teff
I cup grated Parmesan cheese or cheese alternative
Freshly ground black pepper

1. In a medium, heavy saucepan, bring the broth to a boil over
high heat. Stir in the salt, cornmeal, and teff, reduce the heat to
low, and cook, stirring constantly, about 10 minutes. Cover with
the lid, remove from the heat, and let sit about 15 minutes.

2. Stir in the Parmesan and pepper. Serve immediately.

TEFF-CORN POLENTA SQUARES

Press the Teff-Corn Polenta to a ½-inch thickness in a parchment-
lined 13 × 9-inch baking dish. Chill for 2 hours and then cut into
serving-size pieces and fry in olive oil until crispy and brown.

Warm Lentils with Herbs

MAKES 4 SERVINGS

Serve these hearty lentils as a side dish or try a simple but sophisticated presentation by placing slices of your most elegant roast, rack of lamb, or chops on top. Although I use brown lentils here, you may use red or yellow if you wish.

I cup brown lentils
I cup gluten-free, low-sodium chicken broth
¼ cup diced yellow onion
½ teaspoon salt
I garlic clove, minced
2 ripe plum tomatoes, diced
2 tablespoons coarsely chopped fresh basil or thyme or 1½ teaspoons dried
2 tablespoons coarsely chopped fresh flat-leaf parsley or 1½ teaspoons dried
2 tablespoons extra-virgin olive oil
I tablespoon sherry vinegar or Champagne vinegar
Salt and freshly ground black pepper

1. In a medium pan, combine the lentils, broth, onion, salt, and garlic. Bring to a boil over medium heat, reduce the heat to low, and simmer, covered, until the lentils are soft, about 30 minutes.

2. Stir in the tomatoes, basil, parsley, oil, and vinegar and heat to serving temperature, about 5 minutes. Add the salt and pepper to taste. Serve hot.

☀ Black-Eyed Peas with Collard Greens and Rice

MAKES 4 SERVINGS

Black-eyed peas, a staple in the South, are pale-colored beans with a prominent black spot—hence their name. High in calcium, they are often served with collard greens for a nutritious, flavorful dish. You can also add chopped ham, if you wish.

2 tablespoons olive oil
I medium onion, coarsely chopped
I garlic clove, minced
½ pound collard greens
4 cups gluten-free, low-sodium vegetable broth
I (14- to 15-ounce) can black-eyed peas, rinsed and drained
Salt and freshly ground black pepper
I teaspoon apple cider vinegar or sherry vinegar
4 cups hot cooked brown rice

1. In a Dutch oven or other deep, heavy pot with a tight-fitting lid, heat the oil over medium heat. Add the onion and garlic and cook, stirring occasionally, until the onion is soft and translucent, about 5 minutes.

2. While the onion mixture is cooking, discard the stems and center ribs from the collard greens, wash thoroughly, and finely chop the remaining leaves. Add the collards and broth to the onion mixture and simmer until the collards are tender, about 20 minutes.

3. In a small bowl, mash half of the black-eyed peas with a fork. Stir the mashed and whole peas into the onion-collard mixture and simmer until heated through, about 5 minutes. Add the salt and pepper to taste, and stir in the vinegar. Serve over the rice.

Linguine with White Clam Sauce

MAKES 4 SERVINGS

Serve this easy dish with a crisp tossed salad and a loaf of crusty French bread for a quick meal. Remember this dish when you need a meal on the table in 10 minutes, eliminating that 5:00 P.M. "what's for dinner staredown" at the refrigerator.

1 tablespoon extra-virgin olive oil
¼ teaspoon crushed red pepper flakes
1 garlic clove, minced
2 tablespoons coarsely chopped fresh thyme or 1 teaspoon dried
1 teaspoon anchovy paste
½ cup dry white wine
2 (6.5-ounce) cans clams, including juice
¼ teaspoon lemon pepper
1 pound gluten-free linguine
2 tablespoons coarsely chopped fresh flat-leaf parsley
Sweet paprika, for garnish

1. In a deep pot, heat the oil over medium heat. Add the red pepper flakes, garlic, thyme, and anchovy paste, and cook 1 minute. Add the wine, clams, and lemon pepper. Simmer over low heat, uncovered, for 5 minutes.

2. While the sauce simmers, cook the linguine according to the package directions. Drain thoroughly.

3. Transfer the linguine to a large serving bowl and toss gently with the sauce. Garnish with a dash of paprika. Serve immediately.

 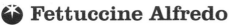

Fettuccine Alfredo

MAKES 4 SERVINGS

My version of this traditionally high-calorie dish uses less-fattening ingredients without compromising the flavor. The type of pasta you use affects the dish's texture—heavier and darker in color if you use Tinkyada pasta; lighter in color if you use Pastariso pasta.

1½ cups low-fat cream cheese or cream cheese alternative
3 tablespoons milk of choice
¼ cup grated Parmesan cheese or cheese alternative
1 small garlic clove, minced
2 tablespoons unsalted butter or buttery spread
4 cups hot cooked gluten-free fettuccine
¼ cup coarsely chopped fresh flat-leaf parsley, for garnish (optional)
1 teaspoon lemon pepper, for garnish (optional)

1. In a food processor, combine the cream cheese, milk, Parmesan, garlic, and butter. Process until the sauce is very smooth.

2. Transfer the sauce to a medium, heavy saucepan and whisk over medium heat until the sauce reaches serving temperature, about 3 to 5 minutes.

3. Serve immediately over the fettuccine, garnished with the parsley and lemon pepper, if using.

HOW TO COOK PASTA

• Use plenty of water 4 cups per 8 ounces of pasta.
• Salt the water liberally after it starts to boil—most pasta is mild and salt brings out its flavor.
• Put the pasta into boiling water and stir constantly until it comes to a boil again to prevent clumping.
• Cook the pasta following the package directions because different brands of gluten-free pasta are made with different grains and therefore cook at different rates.
• Cook the pasta until it feels slightly soft when you bite into it—sometimes called al dente or "to the tooth" in Italian. Remove the pasta immediately from the heat and drain; it will continue to cook from residual heat even after it is out of the boiling water.
• Use cooked gluten-free pasta immediately; it will get mushy and break apart if it sits in the pot or on a buffet table for an extended period of time. Gently stir it into the sauce so you don't tear the pasta.
• Cooked pasta tends to clump together when chilled, but it will separate when rinsed briefly with hot water.

✸ Macaroni and Cheese

☺ MAKES 4 SERVINGS

This traditional comfort-food dish, a classic loved by kids of all ages, is usually off-limits in a gluten-free diet. But today's store-bought, gluten-free pasta allows us to re-create its creamy goodness. The flavor of this all-American favorite is enhanced with hot sauce, dry mustard, and nutmeg—you won't detect their presence, but you will appreciate the overall effect.

3 cups milk of choice
3 tablespoons sweet rice flour*
2 tablespoons unsalted butter or buttery spread
2 cups grated sharp Cheddar cheese or cheese alternative
1 cup grated Monterey Jack, mild white cheese, or cheese alternative
2 tablespoons grated Parmesan cheese or cheese alternative
1 teaspoon hot pepper sauce
½ teaspoon dry mustard
⅛ teaspoon freshly grated nutmeg
2 cups hot cooked gluten-free elbow macaroni
1 cup Plain Bread Crumbs (page 49) or other gluten-free bread crumbs (optional)
Sweet paprika, for garnish

1. Place a rack in the middle of the oven. Preheat the oven to 350°F. Generously grease a 2-quart baking dish.

2. Place all but ¼ cup of the milk in a heavy, medium saucepan. In a small bowl, stir the rice flour with the remaining ¼ cup milk until it is smooth; whisk into the milk in the saucepan. Cook over medium heat, whisking constantly, until the mixture thickens, about 5 to 8 minutes. Add the butter and stir until melted.

3. Remove the pan from the heat and stir in the cheeses, hot pepper sauce, mustard, and nutmeg until the cheeses are completely melted. Add the pasta to the sauce and toss to coat the pasta thoroughly with the cheese sauce. Transfer the mixture to the prepared baking dish.

4. Bake 15 minutes. Sprinkle with the bread crumbs and a dusting of paprika. Bake until the cheese is bubbly and the bread crumbs are browned, about 15 minutes more. For speedier results, place a broiler rack about 6 inches away from the heat source. Preheat the broiler and broil until the bread crumbs are browned and crunchy, about 1 to 2 minutes. Let stand 5 minutes. Serve immediately.

*If using rice or potato milk, increase the sweet rice flour to 4 tablespoons.

Spaghetti with Marinara Sauce

MAKES 12 SERVINGS

Make a big batch of the marinara sauce and freeze it in meal-size portions so all you have to do is boil the pasta and toss with the thawed marinara to have a quick meal for the family.

1 (24-ounce) can tomato juice
2 (6-ounce) cans tomato paste
¼ cup coarsely chopped fresh basil or 2 tablespoons dried
2 tablespoons coarsely chopped fresh flat-leaf parsley or 1 tablespoon dried
2 teaspoons sugar
2 teaspoons coarsely chopped fresh oregano or 1 teaspoon dried
2 teaspoons finely snipped fresh rosemary or 1 teaspoon dried, crushed
1 teaspoon salt, or to taste
½ teaspoon crushed red pepper flakes
½ teaspoon freshly ground black pepper
1 garlic clove, minced
1 bay leaf
2 tablespoons grated Romano cheese or cheese alternative (optional)
1½ pounds gluten-free spaghetti

1. In a Dutch oven or other deep, heavy pot with a tight-fitting lid, whisk together all the ingredients except the spaghetti. Bring to a boil over high heat, reduce the heat to low, and simmer, covered, 30 to 45 minutes. Stir frequently and add ¼ cup water if the sauce appears too dry. Remove the bay leaf and discard.
2. Cook the spaghetti according to package directions (see How to Cook Pasta, page 95). Serve each portion topped with about ⅓ cup marinara sauce.

SPAGHETTI WITH MEATBALLS

Prepare Spaghetti with Marinara Sauce (at left) and serve with this delicious Italian staple.

1 pound lean ground beef or ½ pound ground beef and ½ pound ground pork
¼ cup finely chopped onion
½ cup Plain Bread Crumbs (page 49) or gluten-free store-bought bread crumbs
1 large egg, beaten
4 tablespoons coarsely chopped fresh flat-leaf parsley or 2 tablespoons dried
1 tablespoon coarsely chopped fresh basil or 1½ teaspoons dried
1 teaspoon coarsely chopped fresh oregano or ½ teaspoon dried
½ teaspoon salt
½ teaspoon freshly ground black pepper
¼ teaspoon crushed red pepper flakes (optional)
¼ teaspoon garlic powder
2 tablespoons grated Romano cheese or cheese alternative (optional)

1. Place a rack in the middle of the oven. Preheat the oven to 350°F. Line a 13 × 9-inch baking sheet with aluminum foil. In a large bowl, combine the beef, onion, bread crumbs, egg, parsley, basil, oregano, salt, pepper, red pepper flakes, if using, garlic powder, and Romano, if using.

2. Mix the ingredients well with your hands and shape into 12 meatballs, each about 1½ inches in diameter. Place them on the prepared baking sheet.

3. Bake until the meatballs are nicely browned and firm, about 20 minutes. Remove from the oven and cool 15 minutes on the sheet. Add them to the marinara sauce and serve.

Penne Pasta Primavera

MAKES 4 SERVINGS.

Primavera means "springtime" in Italian and aptly describes this dish because the vegetables used in it are plentiful during the spring. But you can use whatever vegetables you have on hand.

5 spears asparagus, trimmed, cut into 1-inch diagonal slices (about 1 cup)
¼ pound snow peas, trimmed and halved diagonally (about 1 cup)
½ teaspoon salt
4 cups hot cooked gluten-free penne
½ cup Parmesan cheese or cheese alternative
2 tablespoons dry white wine
2 tablespoons rice wine vinegar
1 tablespoon extra-virgin olive oil
1 garlic clove, minced
1 teaspoon onion powder
¼ teaspoon white pepper
1 cup red grape tomatoes or cherry tomatoes, halved
¼ cup coarsely chopped onion, sautéed until tender
¼ cup coarsely chopped fresh flat-leaf parsley

1. Cook the asparagus and snow peas in a pot of boiling, salted water just until barely done, 1 to 2 minutes. Drain and immerse in ice water to stop the cooking process and preserve the color. Transfer the vegetables to a large serving bowl, add the penne, and toss with the Parmesan.

2. In a screw-top jar, combine the wine, vinegar, oil, garlic, onion powder, and pepper and shake vigorously until well blended. Pour over the penne and vegetables and toss to coat thoroughly. Add the tomatoes, onion, and parsley and toss to coat thoroughly. Let stand at room temperature so the flavors blend, about 30 minutes, and serve at room temperature.

Ravioli in Creamy Marinara Sauce

MAKES 4 SERVINGS

Homemade ravioli take a little patience—to roll out the dough, shape it, and fill it—so save this recipe for a day when you have the time. Your reward is delectable ravioli and you can freeze the uncooked ravioli in an airtight food storage bag for up to 3 months.

RAVIOLI
½ cup grated Parmesan cheese or cheese alternative
½ cup ricotta cheese or cream cheese alternative
1 teaspoon Italian seasoning
1 large egg, separated
1 recipe Handmade Pasta (opposite)
1 tablespoon water

CREAMY MARINARA SAUCE
2 cups Marinara Sauce (page 98) or other gluten-free marinara sauce
⅔ cup heavy cream or ½ cup milk of choice

1. Make the ravioli: In a small bowl, mix together the Parmesan, ricotta, Italian seasoning, and egg yolk until smooth; set aside.

2. Roll the dough with a rolling pin to a 12-inch square on a sheet of parchment paper. (Place a damp paper towel under the parchment paper to anchor it.) In a small bowl, whisk together the egg white and water until the egg membrane is totally broken up and brush it on half of the dough. Place half-teaspoonfuls of the cheese filling 2 inches apart on the egg-painted side of the dough.

3. Fold the unpainted half of the dough over the filled portion and seal the edges with your fingers. Press the dough together between the mounds every 2 inches.

4. Cut the ravioli into 2-inch squares with a pastry cutter, following the lines where you've pressed the dough together. Or use a pastry wheel crimper that both cuts and crimps (presses the edges together with a curvy line pattern) the dough at the same time. If the edges are not properly sealed, the filling will fall out when the ravioli are boiled.

5. Make the sauce: In a small pan, heat the marinara sauce over medium heat to serving temperature, about 3 to 5 minutes. Cover and keep warm while cooking the ravioli. Just before serving, stir in the cream and bring to serving temperature again.

6. In a large pot, bring water to a boil over high heat. Salt liberally, add the ravioli, and cook 5 to 10 minutes or until done. Serve immediately with the sauce. (You may also freeze ravioli for later use, if desired.)

HANDMADE PASTA
MAKES 4 SERVINGS

Use this basic recipe to make hand-cut thin noodles and lasagna noodles (or follow the Ravioli in Creamy Marinara Sauce ravioli recipe to make stuffed pasta–like ravioli). Handmade pasta is delicious and cooks quickly because it is fresh, not dried. Be sure to dust white rice flour on the dough to prevent sticking when you roll it.

2 large eggs, at room temperature
¼ cup water
1 tablespoon canola oil
½ cup sorghum flour
½ cup tapioca flour
¼ cup potato starch
½ cup cornstarch
4 teaspoons xanthan gum
½ teaspoon salt
White rice flour, for dusting

1. In a food processor, process the eggs, water, and oil until the eggs are light yellow in color. Add both flours, the potato starch, cornstarch, xanthan gum, and salt. Process until thoroughly blended and the dough forms a ball. Break up the dough into smaller egg-size pieces and process until a ball forms again.

2. Remove the dough and knead it with your hands until smooth. Divide the dough into 2 balls. Cover 1 ball with plastic wrap to keep it from drying out. Place the remaining ball of dough on a 15 × 15-inch sheet of parchment paper dusted with white rice flour. Cover with plastic wrap, using overlapping pieces to cover the parchment paper, and roll the dough with a rolling pin to ⅟₁₆ inch thick or as thin as possible.

3. To make thin noodles: Remove the plastic wrap and use a sharp knife to cut the dough into ¼-inch-wide noodles with a sharp knife or a rolling herb mincer (available at kitchen stores). Repeat with the remaining ball of dough. Use immediately or drape the strips over a pasta-drying rack. To make lasagna noodles: Remove the plastic wrap and use a sharp knife or a pastry crimper (rolling cutter with scalloped edges) to cut the dough into 2-inch-wide strips. Use immediately or drape the strips over a pasta-drying rack.

Potato Gnocchi

MAKES 4 SERVINGS

Gnocchi means "lump" in Italian and is also used to describe Italian dumplings. But gnocchi are most often served like pasta and tossed with melted butter, Parmesan cheese, or marinara sauce. There are many varieties, but this easy version uses mashed potatoes as the base.

2 large russet potatoes, peeled and cut into 1-inch cubes
2 teaspoons salt
2 tablespoons unsalted butter or buttery spread, at room temperature
1 large egg
1 cup Carol's Sorghum Blend (page 14), or more if needed
½ teaspoon xanthan gum

1. In a large pot, place the potatoes and add 1 teaspoon of the salt and enough water to cover. Bring to a boil over high heat, reduce the heat to medium, and cook, covered, until tender but still firm, about 15 minutes. Drain the potatoes and cool 5 minutes. Mash them with a potato ricer, for best results, or with a fork or potato masher.

2. Transfer the potatoes to a large bowl. Beat in the butter and ½ teaspoon salt with an electric mixer on low speed until well blended. Then beat in the egg until well blended, about 1 minute. Cover the bowl tightly with plastic wrap and cool until the potatoes are cool enough to handle, about 15 minutes. Beat in the sorghum blend and xanthan gum on low speed. The dough will appear crumbly, but will form a soft ball when shaped with your hands.

3. Divide the dough into 6 portions, keeping unused portions covered tightly in plastic wrap to prevent it from drying out. On a sheet of wax paper, roll each portion into a long rope with your hands, about ¾ inch in diameter, and cut into 1-inch pieces. To make the gnocchi, hold a piece in the palm of your hand and gently press the tines of a fork into the ball to create indentations.

4. Bring a large pot of water to a boil over high heat. Add the remaining ½ teaspoon salt. Add the gnocchi and cook until they float to the top, about 1 minute, and then cook them 30 seconds more. Remove the gnocchi with a slotted spoon and serve immediately.

MAIN DISHES

POULTRY

Simple Roasted Chicken with Stuffing
Pan-Roasted Chicken Breasts with Apricot-Teriyaki Glaze
Chicken Marsala with Mushrooms
Chicken Cacciatore
Chicken Pot Pie
Chicken-Fried Chicken with White Gravy
Lemon Chicken
Chicken Satay with Peanut Sauce

BEEF, PORK, AND LAMB

Grilled Mustard-Marinated Flank Steak
Chipotle Grilled Steaks
Stuffed Trio of Sweet Peppers
Braised Pot Roast with Vegetables
Barbecued Baby Back Ribs
Pork Carnitas in a Slow Cooker
Grilled Pork Chops with Thyme
Corn Dogs
Oven-Roasted Pork Tenderloin with Sage-Apple-Cranberry
    Relish
Pork Schnitzel
Pan-Grilled Rosemary Lamb Chops

FISH AND SEAFOOD

Sole Piccata
Broiled Soy-Glazed Salmon
Pan-Fried Grouper in Thai Curry Sauce
Mediterranean Fish Fillets Baked in Parcels
Pan-Seared Halibut with Apple-Pear Chutney
Scallop Stir-Fry
Shrimp Étouffée

VEGGIES

Marinated Vegetable Stir-Fry
Vegetable Tempura with Dipping Sauce
Chiles Rellenos

Simple Roasted Chicken with Stuffing

MAKES 4 SERVINGS

I roast a whole chicken frequently because I love it and I use any leftover chicken meat for soups and sandwiches. I also make a chicken broth using the bones and freeze it for later use. The stuffing can also be served with pork chops. You can also double or triple the stuffing recipe and use it for your Thanksgiving turkey.

I (3-pound) chicken
Juice of I lemon
6 cups White Sandwich Yeast Bread (page 48) or other gluten-free
   white bread, cut into I-inch cubes
2 tablespoons unsalted butter or buttery spread
I small onion, finely chopped
2 stalks celery, finely chopped
I teaspoon salt
¼ cup coarsely chopped fresh flat-leaf parsley
2 teaspoons coarsely chopped fresh sage or I teaspoon dried
½ to I cup gluten-free, low-sodium chicken broth
2 teaspoons celery salt or table salt
½ teaspoon freshly ground black pepper
½ cup hot water
Mixed greens, for serving

1. Place a rack in the middle of the oven. Preheat the oven to 400°F. Generously grease a heavy-duty roasting pan, preferably one with a lid.

2. Check the chicken for pin feathers, trim off any extra fat, and pat it dry with paper towels. Squeeze lemon juice all over the chicken and inside the cavity. Set aside while making the stuffing.

3. Place the bread cubes in a large bowl; set aside. In a medium skillet, heat the butter over medium heat until melted. Add the onion, celery, and salt and cook, stirring occasionally, until translucent, about 5 minutes. Add the onion-celery mixture to the bread cubes, along with the parsley and sage and mix with a rubber spatula or your hands until thoroughly blended. Add the broth and stir until the bread cubes are thoroughly moistened. Stuff the chicken cavity with the bread mixture.

(continued on following page)

4. Place the chicken breast-side up on the rack in the prepared baking dish. Pierce the skin on the breast and legs with a fork. Sprinkle the celery salt and pepper on the chicken. Add the water to the pan, cover, and roast until the skin is browned, 1½ to 2 hours. Remove the lid during the last 30 minutes to promote browning. The chicken is done when the juices run clear when the thigh is pierced and the temperature in the thickest part of the thigh and the thickest part of the breast is 170°F on an instant-read thermometer.

5. Remove the pan from the oven and let the chicken sit, covered, on a wire rack for 15 minutes. Transfer the stuffing to a serving bowl, carve the chicken, and serve on a bed of mixed greens. Refrigerate any leftovers for up to 3 days.

Pan-Roasted Chicken Breasts with Apricot-Teriyaki Glaze

MAKES 4 SERVINGS

Sweet apricot jam and savory soy sauce make a delightful glaze on these chicken breasts. Pan-roasting involves browning the chicken breasts in a skillet, then transferring them—skillet and all—to finish cooking in a preheated oven. It's a great timesaver, too, because it frees you up to complete the remainder of the meal.

4 (5-ounce) boneless skinless chicken breast halves
½ teaspoon salt
¼ teaspoon freshly ground black pepper
2 tablespoons canola oil
⅔ cup apricot jam
½ cup fresh orange juice
2 tablespoons Dijon mustard
2 tablespoons wheat-free tamari soy sauce
I teaspoon grated fresh ginger
¼ cup almond slices
I tablespoon sesame seeds
I tablespoon coarsely chopped fresh flat-leaf parsley, for garnish

1. Place a rack in the middle of the oven. Preheat the oven to 350°F. With a meat mallet, pound the chicken breasts between two sheets of plastic wrap to ½-inch thickness. Sprinkle with the salt and pepper.

2. In a large, heavy ovenproof skillet, heat the oil over medium-high heat. Brown the chicken breasts, about 5 minutes per side depending on the size, or until the juice is no longer pink when the centers of the thickest pieces are pierced.

3. While the chicken is browning, mix together the jam, orange juice, mustard, soy sauce, and ginger. Pour over the chicken and bake, uncovered, until the chicken is cooked through, 15 to 20 minutes. The glaze will thicken slightly as the chicken bakes.

4. During the last 5 minutes of baking, spoon the glaze over the chicken breasts and then sprinkle the almonds and sesame seeds over the chicken. Remove the skillet from the oven and transfer the chicken to a serving platter, spooning glaze around the breasts. Garnish with the parsley and serve.

Chicken Marsala with Mushrooms

MAKES 4 SERVINGS

This is a classic Italian dish made with Marsala wine and mushrooms. A hint of nutmeg lends a mysterious but complementary flavor. It is a rich and satisfying dish that will please family or dinner guests, and it's simple enough to make often.

- 1½ pounds thinly sliced boneless skinless chicken breast halves
- ¼ cup cornstarch
- 1 teaspoon salt
- ½ teaspoon freshly ground black pepper
- 2 tablespoons unsalted butter, buttery spread, or olive oil
- 2 garlic cloves, minced
- 1 (8-ounce) can sliced mushrooms, drained
- ⅛ teaspoon freshly grated nutmeg
- 1 cup Marsala wine
- 1 teaspoon cornstarch stirred into 1 tablespoon water (optional)
- 2 tablespoons grated Parmesan cheese or cheese alternative, for garnish

1. With a meat mallet, pound the chicken breasts between two sheets of plastic wrap to ½-inch thickness. In a shallow bowl, dredge the chicken in the cornstarch, then season with the salt and pepper.

2. In a large skillet, heat the butter over medium-high heat. Cook the chicken until deep golden brown and the juice is no longer pink when the centers of the thickest pieces are pierced, about 4 to 5 minutes per side. Remove the chicken from the pan and cover with aluminum foil to keep warm.

3. In the same skillet, add the garlic, mushrooms, nutmeg, and Marsala. Stir to loosen the browned bits from the bottom of the skillet. Bring the mixture to a boil over high heat, reduce the heat to medium-low, and cook until the mixture is reduced by a third. If you prefer a thicker sauce with more body, stir in the cornstarch-water mixture and cook until the mixture thickens, about 1 minute.

4. Return the chicken to the pan and cook until it reaches serving temperature, 1 to 2 minutes. Serve the chicken with the pan juices poured on top and garnished with the Parmesan.

Chicken Cacciatore

MAKES 4 SERVINGS

This easy-to-assemble, one-pot dish blends chicken with tomatoes and Italian herbs for an easy, but hearty entrée. Often called hunter's stew, legend has it that Italian wives prepared it for their husbands to fortify them during hunting season. Serve it on a cold winter's night and your guests will be well fortified for their journey home.

2 tablespoons olive oil
4 (5-ounce) boneless skinless chicken breast halves
1 (8-ounce) can chopped mushroom pieces
½ cup finely chopped red bell pepper
1 small onion, finely diced
1 garlic clove, minced
1 (14- to 15-ounce) can peeled whole tomatoes with juice, coarsely chopped
½ cup dry red wine
2 tablespoons capers, drained and rinsed (optional)
2 tablespoons fresh lemon juice
1 tablespoon tomato paste
4 teaspoons coarsely chopped fresh oregano or 2 teaspoons dried
2 teaspoons coarsely chopped fresh thyme or 1 teaspoon dried
1 teaspoon sugar
½ teaspoon salt
¼ teaspoon crushed red pepper flakes
¼ teaspoon freshly ground black pepper
2 teaspoons cornstarch stirred into 2 tablespoons cold water
4 cups hot cooked gluten-free pasta, such as penne or fusilli

1. In a Dutch oven or other deep, heavy pot with a tight-fitting lid, heat the oil over medium-high heat. Add the chicken breasts and cook until golden brown on all sides, about 5 minutes per side. Transfer the chicken to a plate. Add the mushrooms, red bell pepper, onion, and garlic to the pot. Cook the vegetables, stirring often, until they begin to soften, about 5 minutes.

2. Add the tomatoes with their juice, wine, capers (if using), lemon juice, tomato paste, oregano, thyme, sugar, salt, red pepper flakes, and black pepper, and bring to a boil over high heat. Return the chicken to the skillet, reduce the heat to low and simmer, covered, 30 minutes.

3. Just before serving, stir the cornstarch mixture into the sauce, raise the heat to medium, and stir until the sauce thickens. Serve the sauce over the chicken and the pasta.

Chicken Pot Pie

MAKES 4 SERVINGS

A pot pie is the perfect way to use up leftover cooked chicken. If you prefer a creamy filling, replace half of the chicken broth with heavy cream. Bake it in a casserole dish or in four individual ramekins.

FILLING
- 2 cups cooked chicken, cut into ½-inch pieces
- ½ cup coarsely chopped onion
- ¼ pound broccoli, cut into 1-inch florets (about ½ cup)
- 1 small carrot, thinly sliced
- ¼ cup frozen corn kernels
- ¼ cup frozen green peas
- 1 small cooked russet potato, peeled and cubed
- 1 ripe plum tomato, cut into ½-inch cubes
- 1 tablespoon Dijon mustard
- 1 teaspoon salt
- 2 teaspoons coarsely chopped fresh thyme or 1 teaspoon dried
- 1 teaspoon coarsely chopped fresh rosemary or ½ teaspoon dried, crushed
- ¼ teaspoon dried summer savory, crushed (optional)
- ¼ teaspoon freshly ground black pepper
- ⅛ teaspoon freshly grated nutmeg
- 1 cup gluten-free, low-sodium chicken broth
- 1 tablespoon cornstarch stirred into 2 tablespoons cold water

TOPPING
- 1 cup Carol's Sorghum Blend (page 14)
- 1 teaspoon sugar
- 1 teaspoon baking powder
- ¼ teaspoon baking soda
- 1 teaspoon xanthan gum
- 2 teaspoons coarsely chopped fresh flat-leaf parsley or 1 teaspoon dried
- ¼ teaspoon celery salt
- 2 tablespoons butter or buttery spread, melted
- ½ cup milk of choice
- 1 large egg white

1. Place a rack in the middle of the oven. Preheat the oven to 375°F. Generously grease an 8- or 9-inch round, deep baking dish or 4 ramekins.

2. Make the filling: Place all the filling ingredients in the prepared baking dish and mix together. (At this point, you may refrigerate the filling until you want to bake it—either the next day or that night.)

3. Bake the filling, covered, until the mixture is bubbling, about 30 minutes. Remove from the oven.

(continued on following page)

4. Make the topping: Combine the topping ingredients in a small bowl and whisk together. Drop by tablespoonfuls onto the hot filling. Return the chicken pot pie to the oven and bake until the topping is golden brown and crisp, 20 to 25 minutes. Serve hot.

Chicken-Fried Chicken with White Gravy

MAKES 4 SERVINGS

Chicken-fried steak is an American country favorite, but chicken-fried chicken suits those who prefer chicken to steak. There's something about this dish's crispy coating that we gluten-free folks absolutely crave, but we create it with cornstarch rather than wheat flour.

CHICKEN
- I cup cornstarch
- 2 teaspoons seasoned salt
- ¼ teaspoon freshly ground black pepper
- ½ cup milk of choice
- 2 large eggs
- 4 (5-ounce) boneless skinless chicken breast halves
- ¼ cup canola oil, for frying

GRAVY
- 2½ cups milk of choice
- I tablespoon apple cider vinegar
- 4 teaspoons sweet rice flour
- ½ teaspoon salt
- ½ teaspoon onion powder
- ½ teaspoon freshly ground black pepper

1. Make the chicken: In a shallow bowl, combine the cornstarch, seasoned salt, and pepper. In a separate shallow bowl, whisk the milk and eggs together until the egg membrane is broken up and the mixture is very smooth.

2. With a meat mallet, pound the chicken between two sheets of plastic wrap until it is ¼ to ⅓ inch thick. Dip the chicken first in the cornstarch mixture, then in the egg mixture, then in the cornstarch mixture again. Repeat with each chicken breast.

3. In a large, heavy nonstick skillet, heat the oil over medium-high heat. Fry the chicken until golden brown, 4 to 5 minutes per side, turning only once. If you turn them more than once, the coating will fall off. Remove the chicken to a platter, covering with aluminum foil to keep warm.

4. Make the gravy: Pour off all but 1 tablespoon of the oil from the skillet, leaving the browned bits. Add 2 cups milk and the vinegar to the skillet and cook over medium-high heat. In a small bowl, whisk the rice flour, salt, onion powder, and pepper with the remaining ½ cup milk until very smooth. Pour the milk mixture into the skillet, whisking constantly until the mixture thickens, about 7 to 10 minutes. Pour over the chicken. Serve immediately.

☺ CHICKEN FINGERS

In step 2, cut each pounded chicken breast into ¾-inch-wide strips to create "fingers" before dipping into the flour and egg mixtures and proceeding with the rest of the recipe.

Lemon Chicken

MAKES 4 SERVINGS

This dish is often found in Chinese restaurants, but it is so easy to make it gluten-free at home. Just brown the chicken breasts and then create a simple pan sauce to pour over them.

4 (5-ounce) boneless skinless chicken breast halves
½ cup plus 2 tablespoons cornstarch
½ teaspoon salt
2 tablespoons canola oil
I teaspoon ground ginger
I cup gluten-free, low-sodium chicken broth
2 tablespoons honey
2 tablespoons fresh lemon juice
I tablespoon apple cider vinegar
I teaspoon grated lemon zest
2 tablespoons dried chives or 6 green onions, green parts only, finely chopped diagonally, for garnish
4 cups hot cooked basmati rice, for serving

1. Pat the chicken breasts dry with paper towels. With a meat mallet, pound the chicken between two sheets of plastic wrap until slightly flattened.

2. In a medium bowl, combine the ½ cup cornstarch and the salt. Dip each chicken breast in the cornstarch mixture to coat thoroughly.

3. In a large, heavy skillet, heat the oil over medium-high heat. Cook the chicken breasts until nicely browned and cooked through and the juice is no longer pink when the centers of the thickest pieces are pierced, about 5 minutes per side. Remove from the skillet and cover with aluminum foil to keep warm.

4. Stir the remaining 2 tablespoons cornstarch and the ginger into ¼ cup broth until smooth. Add to the skillet, along with the remaining ¾ cup broth and the honey. Cook over medium heat, stirring frequently, until the mixture thickens and comes to a boil. Remove from the heat. Stir in the lemon juice, vinegar, and lemon zest.

5. Cut each chicken breast into 4 slices, slightly at a diagonal. Arrange on a serving plate and pour the sauce over the chicken. Sprinkle with the chives and serve immediately with the rice.

Chicken Satay with Peanut Sauce

MAKES 4 SERVINGS AS A MAIN COURSE OR 8 AS AN APPETIZER

A satay is a strip of marinated meat threaded on a skewer and grilled. It makes a delightful meal served on a bed of cooked rice. Or serve it as an appetizer, with the peanut sauce as a dip.

CHICKEN

- 1 cup unsweetened canned coconut milk
- 1 tablespoon wheat-free tamari soy sauce
- 1 tablespoon sugar
- 1 teaspoon sesame oil
- 1 teaspoon grated fresh ginger
- 1 teaspoon ground coriander
- ½ teaspoon ground turmeric
- ½ teaspoon ground coriander
- ¼ teaspoon ground cumin
- 2 pounds boneless skinless chicken breast halves, cut into ½-inch slices

PEANUT SAUCE

- ½ cup smooth peanut butter
- 3 tablespoons wheat-free, low-sodium tamari soy sauce
- 1 small garlic clove, minced
- ¼ teaspoon crushed red pepper flakes
- 1½ tablespoons packed dark brown sugar
- Juice of 1 lime
- ¼ cup hot water
- 1 tablespoon finely chopped peanuts, for garnish

1. Make the chicken: Combine all the ingredients except the chicken in a heavy-duty food storage bag. Add the chicken and refrigerate 2 hours. Soak 8 bamboo skewers in water for 10 minutes. Remove the chicken from the marinade (discard the marinade) and thread 3 to 4 chicken pieces on each bamboo skewer, stretching out the meat to fill the skewer. Place a barbecue grill about 5 to 6 inches away from the heat source. Preheat the grill to high heat. Grill the skewers until the chicken is browned and cooked through, 4 to 5 minutes.

2. Make the sauce: In a food processor or blender, combine the peanut butter, soy sauce, garlic, red pepper flakes, brown sugar, and lime juice. Puree until well combined. With the motor running, add enough of the hot water to make a thin sauce. Pour the sauce into a serving bowl and garnish with the peanuts. Serve immediately with the chicken.

Grilled Mustard-Marinated Flank Steak

MAKES 4 SERVINGS

Flavorful marinades like this one not only boost the flavor, but also tenderize this economical cut of meat. It is very important to slice flank steak on the diagonal (across the grain, not with the grain) to assure that every bite is as tender as possible.

¼ cup red wine vinegar
¼ cup fresh lemon juice
2 tablespoons olive oil
2 tablespoons packed light brown sugar
2 tablespoons Dijon mustard
I large garlic clove, minced
I teaspoon salt
2 teaspoons coarsely chopped fresh oregano or I teaspoon dried
Dash of hot pepper sauce
I pound flank steak

1. In a medium bowl, whisk together the vinegar, lemon juice, oil, sugar, mustard, garlic, salt, oregano, and hot pepper sauce until thoroughly combined. Pour into a heavy-duty food storage bag. Add the flank steak and marinate at least overnight and up to 24 hours.

2. Place a barbecue grill about 6 inches away from the heat source. Preheat the grill to medium-high heat. Remove the steaks from the marinade (discard the marinade); pat dry. Grill the steaks 3 to 4 minutes, then turn the steaks and cook on the other side, about 3 minutes for rare, 4 minutes for medium-rare. To check for doneness, make a small cut in the thickest part. For longer cooking, move the steaks to a cooler part of the grill.

3. Transfer the steaks from the grill to a plate and cover with aluminum foil to keep warm; let stand 10 minutes. Slice diagonally and serve warm.

Chipotle Grilled Steaks

MAKES 4 SERVINGS

If you like flavorful steaks—but flavored with an extra boost from bold ingredients such as chipotle chile powder—try this very easy idea.

4 (4-ounce) filet mignon or New York strip steaks
1 tablespoon Montreal steak seasoning or seasoning of choice
¼ teaspoon chipotle chile powder
Salt and freshly ground black pepper

1. Pat the beef dry with paper towels. Combine the seasoning and chile powder and rub it on both sides of the steaks. Let the steaks stand at room temperature for 15 minutes.

2. Place a barbecue grill about 6 inches away from the heat source. Preheat the grill to medium-high heat. Grill the steaks 4 to 5 minutes. Turn the meat over and cook on the other side, about 4 minutes for rare, 5 to 6 minutes for medium-rare. To check for doneness, make a small cut in the thickest part. For longer cooking, move the steaks to a cooler part of the grill.

3. Transfer the steaks to a plate, covering with aluminum foil to keep warm; let stand 5 to 10 minutes. Sprinkle with salt and pepper to taste, and serve immediately.

Stuffed Trio of Sweet Peppers

MAKES 6 SERVINGS

Although this is a home-style dish, the colorful peppers look very elegant nestled on a bed of white basmati rice. Use for everyday meals or a lovely dish for guests who like comfort food.

6 medium bell peppers (2 red, 2 yellow, 2 green)
½ pound lean ground beef
2 cups Marinara Sauce (page 98) or other gluten-free marinara sauce
3 cups cooked white rice
1 small onion, finely chopped
1 teaspoon coarsely chopped fresh oregano or ½ teaspoon dried
1 teaspoon coarsely chopped fresh thyme or ½ teaspoon dried
½ teaspoon salt
½ teaspoon freshly ground black pepper
1 garlic clove, minced
4 cups hot cooked white basmati rice

1. Halve each pepper lengthwise, from the stem to the base. Remove the seeds and cut off the stem. Place on a plate and cook in the microwave oven on high, covered with wax paper, 5 minutes. Remove and let cool. Coat a 13 x 9-inch glass baking dish with cooking spray; set aside.

2. In a heavy skillet, cook the ground beef over medium-high heat until nicely browned and the liquid has evaporated, about 5 minutes. Stir in 1 cup marinara sauce, the cooked rice, onion, oregano, thyme, salt, black pepper, and garlic. Spoon the mixture into the peppers. Spoon any leftover mixture around the peppers. (Or freeze to spoon over white rice later for a quick meal.) You may prepare this dish the night before; cover and refrigerate to bake the next day.

3. Place a rack in the middle of the oven. Preheat the oven to 375°F. Bake, covered, until the sauce is bubbling, about 20 minutes. Remove from the oven. Heat the remaining 1 cup marinara sauce to serving temperature over medium heat, about 5 minutes, and drizzle over the stuffed peppers. Serve on a bed of the hot cooked basmati rice.

Braised Pot Roast with Vegetables

MAKES 4 SERVINGS

Braising involves browning, then simmering meat in a covered pot of liquid that breaks down the collagen and increases the meat's tenderness. Cook this mouthwatering roast on the weekend, and use the leftovers for sandwiches and casseroles during the week.

1 (2-pound) boneless chuck roast, trimmed of excess fat
½ teaspoon salt
½ teaspoon freshly ground black pepper
1 tablespoon canola oil
1 medium onion, diced
1 garlic clove, minced
1 (14- to 15-ounce) can petite diced tomatoes, with juice
¼ cup red wine vinegar
1 tablespoon firmly packed light brown sugar
1 bay leaf
1 (3-inch) strip orange rind
1 teaspoon coarsely chopped fresh thyme or ½ teaspoon dried
1 cup gluten-free, low-sodium beef broth
2 cups baby carrots
1 pound very small red potatoes, scrubbed, or 4 medium red potatoes, scrubbed and quartered
1½ tablespoons cornstarch stirred into 2 tablespoons cold water
1 tablespoon coarsely chopped fresh flat-leaf parsley, for garnish

1. Place a rack in the middle of the oven. Preheat the oven to 350°F. Pat the beef dry with paper towels and sprinkle with the salt and pepper on all sides.

2. In a Dutch oven or other deep, heavy pot with a tight-fitting lid, heat the oil over medium-high heat. Cook the beef until browned on all sides, about 5 minutes. Transfer the beef to a plate and set aside. Add the onion and garlic to the Dutch oven, and cook over moderate heat, stirring, until the onion is golden, about 5 minutes. Stir in the tomatoes with their juice, vinegar, sugar, bay leaf, orange rind, thyme, and broth. Carefully place the roast in the liquid and bring the mixture to a boil over high heat.

3. Remove the roast from the heat and transfer to the oven. Cook, covered, 1 hour. Add the carrots and potatoes and continue cooking, covered, 45 minutes more.

4. Transfer the beef and vegetables to a plate and let stand, covered with aluminum foil, for 10 minutes. If you wish to serve the beef with gravy, skim the fat from the top of the cooking liquid and discard the bay leaf and orange rind. Bring the liquid to a boil over high heat. Whisking constantly, add enough of the cornstarch mixture to the boiling liquid to thicken the gravy to the desired consistency. Simmer the gravy over medium heat, stirring occasionally, for 1 minute more. Add additional salt and pepper, if desired. Slice the beef, arrange on a serving platter, and transfer the vegetables to the platter. Spoon some of the gravy over the beef and serve the remaining gravy on the side. Garnish the beef with the parsley. Serve hot.

Barbecued Baby Back Ribs

MAKES 12 SERVINGS

Serve this all-American favorite with down-home sides like Black-Eyed Peas with Collard Greens and Rice (page 93) and creamed corn. You control the heat in this flavorful sauce by how much chili powder and crushed red pepper flakes you use.

RIBS
8 pounds baby back pork ribs (about 6 or 7 slabs)
Salt and freshly ground black pepper

SAUCE
1 (8-ounce) can tomato sauce
¼ cup red wine vinegar
¼ cup molasses (not blackstrap)
2 tablespoons packed light brown sugar
2 tablespoons grated fresh onion
1 tablespoon gluten-free Worcestershire sauce
½ to 1 teaspoon crushed red pepper flakes
2 teaspoons coarsely chopped fresh oregano or 1 teaspoon dried
½ teaspoon freshly ground black pepper
¼ to ½ teaspoon chili powder
½ teaspoon salt
1 garlic clove, minced

1. Make the ribs: Place an oven rack in the middle of the oven. Preheat the oven to 250°F. Sprinkle the meaty side of the ribs with salt and pepper to taste. Wrap the ribs in aluminum foil and bake for 6 to 7 hours. (This step can be done the day before. Cover the cooked ribs and refrigerate.)

2. Make the sauce: In a small saucepan, combine all the sauce ingredients. Bring to a boil over high heat, reduce the heat to low, and simmer 10 to 15 minutes or until the sauce is reduced by one-third. This will be a fairly thin sauce, meant for brushing on the meat in a thin glaze and served as a light sauce at mealtime.

3. Place a barbecue grill about 5 to 6 inches away from the heat source. Preheat the grill to low heat. Heat the ribs to serving temperature, bone-side down, about 20 to 30 minutes. During the last 10 minutes of heating, brush the sauce over the ribs. Serve immediately. Transfer the remaining sauce to a small pitcher and serve with the meal.

☺ Pork Carnitas in a Slow Cooker

MAKES 4 SERVINGS

Carnitas is Spanish for "little meats." Pork tenderloin works great since there are no bones and virtually no waste, but pork shoulder also works well. Serve this dish on top of polenta, in fajitas, or in tacos for the kids.

1 (1-pound) pork tenderloin or pork shoulder, trimmed of excess fat
½ cup gluten-free, low-sodium chicken broth
½ cup gluten-free salsa
1 tablespoon tomato paste
½ teaspoon ground coriander
½ teaspoon salt
¼ teaspoon garlic powder
¼ teaspoon chipotle chile powder
¼ teaspoon freshly ground black pepper

1. Place a rack in the middle of the oven. Preheat the oven to 325°F. Cut the pork tenderloin into ½-inch chunks and add to a slow cooker that has been coated with cooking spray.

2. Combine the remaining ingredients in a medium bowl, pour over the pork and cover. Cook 6 hours in a slow cooker on low heat.

3. Serve the pork as a main dish, spooning the sauce over it. Or shred the pork and serve it as a filling for tacos, using the remaining liquid as a sauce.

SLOW-COOKER TIPS

• Since slow cookers don't brown meat or poultry, browning it in a skillet before putting it in the slow cooker vastly improves its flavor and appearance.

• Choose a slow cooker with a removable insert so you can wash it in the dishwasher. Or you might try the new disposable plastic liners.

• Don't lift the lid to take a peek. Not only does that break the vacuum seal between the lid and the insert that keeps in the heat, but precious heat escapes and this prolongs the cooking time. If your recipe says to stir during cooking, then do it. Otherwise, leave the lid alone.

• Don't set a hot insert on a cold surface such as a granite countertop or run cold water into it; the shock could break it. Don't use harsh abrasives to clean it either.

• Wondering what to cook in your slow cooker? Try spaghetti sauce, stews, ribs, bean soups, whole grains (especially those that take a long time to cook such as brown rice or sorghum).

Grilled Pork Chops with Thyme

MAKES 4 SERVINGS

Fresh thyme elevates an ordinary pork chop to new and attractive culinary heights, but use any fresh herb you like such as sage, oregano, or tarragon. For a tangy variation, serve with the Minted Pineapple Salsa, below.

4 (4-ounce) pork chops
½ teaspoon salt
¼ teaspoon freshly ground black pepper
2 teaspoons coarsely chopped fresh thyme

1. Sprinkle the pork chops with the salt and pepper.

2. Place a barbecue grill about 6 inches away from the heat source. Heat the grill to medium heat. Grill the pork chops on one side until lightly browned, about 5 minutes. Turn and sprinkle evenly with the thyme. Continue grilling the pork chops until browned and no longer pink, about another 3 to 4 minutes, depending on thickness. Serve hot.

MINTED PINEAPPLE SALSA

The sweetness of the pineapple in this salsa balances the vinegar's acidity and the crushed red pepper's heat. It adds appetizing color to these pork chops, but can also be used on chicken or fish.

1 (8-ounce) can pineapple tidbits, drained
¼ cup diced red onion
2 tablespoons diced red bell pepper
1 tablespoon rice vinegar
1 tablespoon honey or agave nectar
1 teaspoon olive oil
¼ teaspoon salt
¼ teaspoon freshly ground black pepper
3 tablespoons coarsely chopped fresh mint
⅛ teaspoon crushed red pepper flakes (optional)

In a small bowl, combine the pineapple, red onion, bell pepper, vinegar, honey, oil, salt, black pepper, mint, and red pepper flakes, if using.

☺ Corn Dogs

MAKES 6 SERVINGS

Kids love corn dogs, which are simply skewered hot dogs that are covered in a deep-fried cornmeal batter. Prepare the batter in a tall, narrow jar or measuring cup to make it easier to coat the skewered hot dog; use wood skewers, which won't burn your fingers; and fry the corn dogs in a wide, shallow skillet (rather than a tall, narrow pot) to make it easier to quickly immerse the whole corn dog.

I cup gluten-free yellow cornmeal
½ cup Carol's Sorghum Blend (page 14)
I tablespoon sugar
½ teaspoon baking soda
¼ teaspoon salt
¾ cup milk of choice
I tablespoon apple cider vinegar
I large egg
6 gluten-free hot dogs
¼ cup white rice flour, for dusting
Peanut oil, for frying

1. In a tall, narrow jar or measuring cup, whisk together the cornmeal, sorghum blend, sugar, baking soda, and salt. In a small bowl or measuring cup, whisk together the milk, vinegar, and egg until all of the egg membrane is broken up. Whisk the milk mixture into the dry ingredients until the batter is very smooth. Let the batter stand 5 minutes. It should be the consistency of pancake batter, thick enough to coat a spoon. If the batter is too stiff, add water, a tablespoon at a time, to thin slightly.

2. Insert a wood skewer into the end of each hot dog. Pat the hot dogs dry with paper towels and dust them with rice flour.

3. Heat 3 inches of the oil in a wide, shallow skillet. Holding the end of the skewer, dip the hot dog in the batter to coat it thoroughly. Immerse the coated hot dog in the oil and fry until lightly browned, turning if necessary to make sure all of the batter is browned, about 3 to 5 minutes.

4. Remove the corn dog from the oil and drain on paper towels. Serve immediately.

MINI–CORN DOGS

1. For kid-size corn dogs, assemble the batter as directed in step 1 but use a wide, shallow bowl.

2. Insert round wooden toothpicks into 24 gluten-free cocktail franks (or 8 hot dogs cut into thirds), and dust with rice flour.

3. Heat the oil to a depth of 3 inches in a small, narrow, heavy saucepan. Gently ease no more than 3 mini–corn dogs at a time into the oil (toothpick and all) and fry until lightly browned, about 1 to 2 minutes. Watch carefully because they will cook very quickly. Remove the corn dogs from the oil with a slotted spoon and drain on paper towels. Serve immediately.

Oven-Roasted Pork Tenderloin with Sage-Apple-Cranberry Relish
MAKES 4 SERVINGS

Sage is a natural flavor partner for pork; this dish takes advantage of that relationship and heightens the flavor with Granny Smith apples—another ingredient that complements pork.

PORK TENDERLOIN
- I tablespoon dry mustard
- I teaspoon dried sage, rubbed
- I teaspoon salt
- ½ teaspoon freshly ground black pepper
- ¼ teaspoon cayenne pepper
- I (I-pound) pork tenderloin
- I tablespoon canola oil

RELISH
- I large Granny Smith apple, cored and diced
- ¼ cup dried cranberries
- ¼ cup diced red onion
- 2 large fresh sage leaves, finely chopped
- I tablespoon coarsely chopped fresh chives
- I tablespoon apple cider vinegar
- I tablespoon honey
- Salt and freshly ground black pepper

1. Place a rack in the middle of the oven. Preheat the oven to 375°F.

2. Make the tenderloin: In a small bowl, stir together the mustard, sage, salt, pepper, and cayenne. Pat the tenderloin dry with paper towels and press the mustard mixture on all sides of the pork.

3. In a medium, heavy, ovenproof skillet, heat the oil over medium heat. Add the tenderloin and cook until browned on all sides, about 5 minutes. Cover the skillet with an ovenproof lid and transfer to the oven.

4. Roast the pork until the internal temperature reaches 145°F to 150°F when an instant-read thermometer is inserted into the center. Remove from the oven and let stand, covered, 10 minutes.

5. Make the relish: In a bowl, combine the apple, cranberries, onion, sage, chives, vinegar, honey, and salt and pepper to taste, and toss thoroughly. Slice the pork into 1½-inch slices and serve with the relish.

Pork Schnitzel

MAKES 4 SERVINGS

This traditional European dish satisfies our cravings for food that's crispy and crunchy. I serve it with mashed potatoes and cooked red cabbage.

I (1-pound) pork tenderloin, cut into ¼-inch slices
½ cup cornstarch
I teaspoon seasoned salt
¼ teaspoon freshly ground black pepper
2 large eggs, thoroughly beaten
I cup Plain Bread Crumbs (page 49) or other gluten-free bread crumbs
¼ cup canola oil, plus more as needed
Additional salt and freshly ground pepper (optional)
I lemon, quartered

1. Place a rack in the middle of the oven. Preheat the oven to 180°F. Line a 15 x 10-inch baking sheet with aluminum foil and lightly coat with cooking spray.

2. Place the pork slices in a single layer in a heavy-duty food storage bag. With the smooth side of a meat mallet, pound the pork to a ¼-inch thickness. Cut the bag open with kitchen scissors, leaving the pounded pork intact.

3. In a shallow bowl, combine the cornstarch, seasoned salt, and pepper. Place the eggs in a separate shallow bowl and the bread crumbs in a third shallow bowl.

4. Dip each pork slice into the cornstarch mixture, then into the eggs, and finally into the bread crumbs.

5. In a large, nonstick (gray, not black) skillet, heat the oil over medium-high heat. Cook the pork, a few pieces at a time, until golden brown, about 5 to 7 minutes per side. Remove the browned pork from the skillet and keep warm in the oven until all the cutlets are cooked. Add salt and pepper to taste, if desired. Serve immediately with a squeeze of lemon.

Pan-Grilled Rosemary Lamb Chops

MAKES 4 SERVINGS

Rosemary works well with lamb in this simple main dish. The chops can be ready in less than 10 minutes, so have all the remaining dishes ready before you prepare the lamb.

2 tablespoons extra-virgin olive oil
2 tablespoons minced fresh rosemary leaves, divided
8 loin lamb chops (about 6 ounces each), trimmed of excess fat
½ teaspoon salt, or to taste
¼ teaspoon freshly ground black pepper, or to taste
2 garlic cloves, minced
½ cup gluten-free, low-sodium chicken broth
Additional salt and freshly ground pepper to taste

1. In a large skillet, heat the oil and 1 tablespoon of the rosemary over medium-high heat. Pat the lamb chops dry with paper towels and sprinkle with salt and pepper.

2. Lay the chops in the pan and cook about 4 minutes per side, turning once, until the internal temperature reads 125°F on an instant-read thermometer inserted into the side of the lamb. When the lamb is cooked on each side, stand the chops on their edges and brown, about 2 minutes more. Reduce the heat if needed so the browned bits remaining in the pan don't burn. Transfer the chops to a plate and cover with foil.

3. Pour off all but 1 tablespoon fat from the skillet. Add the garlic, tilting the skillet to keep the garlic submerged in the fat, and cook over low heat until golden, about 1 minute. Add the broth, stirring up the browned bits from the bottom of the pan, and simmer over high heat until the mixture reduces slightly.

4. Pour the sauce over the lamb chops, sprinkle with the remaining rosemary, and season with additional salt and pepper to taste. Serve immediately.

Sole Piccata

MAKES 4 SERVINGS

Piccata is an Italian dish, and the word itself translates to "piquant," which is fitting due to the tartness of the lemon juice, capers, and wine, although the flavors ultimately balance out beautifully. Sole is quite thin and it will cook very quickly, so have any other dishes ready to serve before you start to prepare this one.

¼ cup white rice flour
¼ teaspoon salt
¼ teaspoon freshly ground black pepper
4 (6-ounce) sole fillets
2 tablespoons unsalted butter, buttery spread, or olive oil
¼ cup dry white wine
¼ cup fresh lemon juice
I tablespoon capers, rinsed and drained
I tablespoon coarsely chopped fresh flat-leaf parsley
I lemon, quartered, for garnish

1. In a shallow bowl, combine the rice flour, salt, and pepper. Pat the sole dry with paper towels and dredge in the flour mixture. Shake off any excess flour.

2. In a large, nonstick (gray, not black) skillet, heat I tablespoon of the butter over medium-high heat. Add the fish and cook until the fish flakes easily with a fork, I to 2 minutes per side. Transfer the fish to a warm serving platter and cover with aluminum foil.

3. Add the wine and lemon juice to the skillet and bring to a boil over high heat; simmer 30 seconds. Add the remaining I tablespoon butter and stir until slightly thickened. Add the capers and parsley and bring the sauce to serving temperature over medium heat. Pour the sauce over the fish and serve immediately, with fresh lemon wedges for garnish.

Broiled Soy-Glazed Salmon

MAKES 4 SERVINGS

Salmon is flavorful any way you cook it, but this broiled version is extremely easy. You can also grill it, if you wish. For a quick meal, serve it with basmati rice and steamed broccoli, or for lunch or a light dinner serve with lightly dressed greens.

¼ cup wheat-free tamari soy sauce
2 tablespoons honey
I tablespoon unseasoned rice vinegar
I tablespoon ground ginger
¼ teaspoon cayenne pepper
⅛ teaspoon freshly ground black pepper
4 (4-ounce) salmon fillets

1. In a large, shallow bowl, combine the soy sauce, honey, vinegar, ginger, cayenne, and black pepper. Add the salmon, flesh-side down, and marinate, refrigerated, for 2 hours.

2. Place a broiler rack about 6 inches away from the heat source. Preheat the broiler. Remove the salmon from the marinade and discard the marinade. Broil the salmon, skin-side down, until the fish is just barely opaque when cut in the thickest part or when it flakes easily with a fork, 8 to 10 minutes, depending on the thickness of the fillets. Serve immediately.

Pan-Fried Grouper in Thai Curry Sauce

MAKES 4 SERVINGS

The heat in this dish comes from the green curry paste. Start with 1 teaspoon and taste the sauce before adding any more. This dish illustrates how many ethnic foods are easily made gluten-free.

RICE
- 2 cups water
- 1 cup white rice
- ½ teaspoon salt
- ¼ teaspoon unsalted butter, buttery spread, or canola oil

SAUCE
- ¼ cup finely snipped fresh chives
- 1 tablespoon gluten-free Asian fish sauce
- 1 tablespoon honey
- 1 to 2 teaspoons gluten-free Thai green curry paste
- 1 teaspoon ground ginger
- 1 teaspoon olive oil
- 1 teaspoon grated lemon zest
- 1 teaspoon grated lime zest
- ¼ teaspoon turmeric
- 1 garlic clove, minced
- 1 (14- to 15-ounce) can unsweetened coconut milk
- ⅛ teaspoon salt, or more to taste
- 1 whole lime or lemon, quartered, for garnish

GROUPER
- 1 tablespoon olive oil
- 4 (4-ounce) grouper or red snapper fillets
- ⅛ teaspoon salt
- ⅛ teaspoon freshly ground black pepper
- ¼ cup coarsely chopped fresh cilantro, for garnish (optional)

1. Make the rice: In a medium saucepan, bring the water to a boil over high heat. Add the rice, salt, and butter, cover, and simmer over low heat until the rice is done, about 20 minutes. Remove from the heat and keep warm.

2. Make the sauce: In a separate medium saucepan, combine all the sauce ingredients and simmer, uncovered, over medium heat, stirring often, for about 10 minutes. The mixture will thicken slightly.

3. Make the grouper: In a medium, nonstick (gray, not black) skillet, heat the oil over medium-high heat. Sprinkle both sides of the grouper with the salt and pepper. Cook the grouper over medium-high heat until the crumbs are golden and the fish is just barely opaque when cut in the thickest part or flakes easily with a fork, 8 to 10 minutes, depending on the thickness of the fish.

4. For each serving, place ½ cup sauce in each of 4 soup bowls. Add ½ cup rice and 1 fillet. Garnish with the cilantro, if using.

Mediterranean Fish Fillets Baked in Parcels

MAKES 4 SERVINGS

The classic French technique of cooking en papillote or "in small packages" makes a beautiful presentation that's fun to unwrap. This is an especially nice choice for company since you can assemble the packets the night before and bake them just before dinner, leaving you time to concentrate on other dishes. Cod, flounder, sole, or red snapper can be used in this dish.

¼ cup unsalted butter or buttery spread, at room temperature, or olive oil
¼ cup blend coarsely chopped fresh chervil, chives, flat-leaf parsley, and thyme
Grated zest and juice of 1 lemon
½ teaspoon salt
½ teaspoon freshly ground black pepper
4 (12-inch-square) sheets parchment paper
4 (5-ounce) white fish fillets
1 (6.5-ounce) jar marinated artichokes, drained
1 cup cherry tomatoes, halved

1. In a small bowl, mash the butter, herbs, lemon zest and juice, salt, and pepper together until smooth. Refrigerate until firm, about 1 hour.

2. Place a rack in the middle of the oven. Preheat the oven to 425°F.

3. Arrange 4 pieces of the parchment paper on a flat work surface. Lay a piece of sole on top of each piece of parchment. Top each fillet with one-quarter of the butter-herb mixture, one-quarter of the drained artichoke hearts, and one-quarter of the tomatoes. Bring two edges of the parchment paper together and crimp or fold together to seal. Twist the ends together to seal. (Refrigerate at this point overnight or proceed to baking.) Place the packets on a rimmed 13 × 9-inch baking sheet. Coat the packets with cooking spray.

4. Bake 15 to 20 minutes if chilled, 12 to 15 minutes if not chilled. The packets will puff up and brown. Remove from the oven and place each packet on a serving plate. Slowly cut open the packets with kitchen scissors to allow the steam to release gently. Serve immediately.

Pan-Seared Halibut with Apple-Pear Chutney

MAKES 4 SERVINGS

This dish is especially enticing as the aroma of scented apples fills the air. If you prefer food less spicy, omit the chili powder.

HALIBUT
   4 (4-ounce) halibut fillets
   I tablespoon chili powder
   ¼ teaspoon salt
   ¼ teaspoon freshly ground black pepper
   I tablespoon olive oil

CHUTNEY
   I tablespoon unsalted butter, buttery spread, or canola oil
   I ripe Bosc pear, peeled, cored, and cut into ½-inch dice
   I small tart apple such as Granny Smith, peeled, cored, and cut into ½-inch slices
   ¼ cup coarsely chopped white onion
   2 tablespoons apple cider vinegar
   I tablespoon fresh lemon juice
   I tablespoon honey
   I tablespoon dried cranberries
   I garlic clove, minced
   ⅛ teaspoon ground cinnamon
   ⅛ teaspoon freshly grated nutmeg
   ⅛ teaspoon ground allspice
   ⅛ teaspoon ground ginger
   Salt and freshly ground black pepper to taste

1. Make the halibut: Pat the halibut fillets dry with a paper towel. Mix the chili powder, salt, and pepper together and press onto both sides of the halibut. Set aside.

2. Make the chutney: In a small, heavy saucepan, heat the butter over medium heat. Add the pear and apple and cook, covered, until slightly softened, about 5 minutes. Add the onion, vinegar, lemon juice, honey, cranberries, garlic, cinnamon, nutmeg, allspice, ginger, salt, and pepper and cook over medium heat until the mixture comes to a boil. Remove from the heat and let stand, covered, while cooking the halibut.

3. In a heavy, nonstick (gray, not black) skillet, heat the oil over medium-high heat. Cook the halibut until the crumbs are golden and the fish is just barely opaque when cut in the thickest part or flakes easily with a fork, 8 to 10 minutes, depending on the thickness of the fish. Serve the halibut topped with the chutney.

Scallop Stir-Fry

MAKES 4 SERVINGS

Stir-fries are a creative way to blend delicious flavors, interesting textures, and appealing colors. For added interest, cut the vegetables in differing shapes—the onion, carrots, and snow peas in diagonals and the red bell pepper in long, narrow strips. If scallops aren't available, use shrimp instead.

1 tablespoon olive oil
1 teaspoon sesame oil
3 green onions, diagonally cut into 1-inch pieces
2 medium carrots, diagonally cut into ½-inch pieces
1 cup fresh snow peas, cut in half diagonally
1 small red bell pepper, cut into ¼-inch strips
1 small yellow bell pepper, cut into ¼-inch strips
¼ cup wheat-free tamari soy sauce
¼ cup fresh lemon juice
¼ cup water
1 tablespoon grated lemon zest
1 tablespoon honey or agave nectar
½ teaspoon crushed red pepper flakes
2 garlic cloves, minced
1 teaspoon grated fresh ginger
1 tablespoon cornstarch
1 pound cooked scallops
4 cups hot cooked brown rice
Additional green onion and lemon peel strips, for garnish

1. In a heavy skillet, heat the olive oil and sesame oil over medium-high heat and add the onions and carrots. Cook, stirring constantly, until crisp-tender, 3 to 5 minutes. Add the snow peas and bell peppers and cook, stirring constantly, a minute more.

2. In a small bowl, whisk together the soy sauce, lemon juice, water, lemon zest, honey, red pepper flakes, garlic, ginger, and cornstarch until smooth. Reduce the heat to medium, stir the sauce into the vegetables, and cook, stirring constantly, just until thickened.

3. Add the scallops to the skillet and simmer gently, without stirring, until they are heated through, about 3 to 4 minutes. Serve immediately over the rice. Garnish with the additional green onions and lemon strips.

Shrimp Étouffée

MAKES 4 SERVINGS

In French, the word *étouffée* means "smothered." The dish is similar to gumbo but is spicier, thicker, and uses a darker roux—which is surprisingly easy to make. Taste the étouffée before serving to determine whether more spices and salt and pepper are needed.

2 tablespoons sorghum flour
2 tablespoons cornstarch
¼ cup canola oil
½ cup finely diced onion
1 stalk celery, finely diced
¼ cup finely diced green bell pepper
1 garlic clove, minced
1 (¼-pound) link gluten-free andouille sausage, cut into ¼-inch slices
1 (8-ounce) bottle clam broth
1 cup dry white wine or gluten-free, low-sodium chicken broth
1 cup petite diced tomatoes, with juice
1 tablespoon gluten-free Worcestershire sauce
2 teaspoons packed light brown sugar
¼ cup coarsely chopped fresh flat-leaf parsley
½ teaspoon gluten-free Creole seasoning
½ teaspoon coarsely chopped fresh thyme or ¼ teaspoon dried
1 bay leaf
½ pound cooked medium shrimp, peeled and deveined

1. In a 10-inch cast-iron skillet, sift together the sorghum flour and cornstarch. Add the oil and whisk until smooth before turning on the heat. Cook over medium-low heat, constantly scraping back and forth with a flat metal spatula, rather than stirring, 30 to 35 minutes. The roux will darken to light beige; continue scraping back and forth as the roux gradually becomes dark brown. Add the onion, celery, bell pepper, and garlic and cook, scraping back and forth occasionally with the spatula, until the onion and bell pepper are softened, 2 to 3 minutes. Remove the skillet from the heat.

2. In a small skillet, cook the sausage over medium heat until browned, 2 to 3 minutes. Add the sausage to the onion-pepper mixture, along with the broth, wine, tomatoes with their juice, Worcestershire sauce, sugar, parsley, Creole seasoning, thyme, and bay leaf. Increase the heat to medium-high and bring to a boil. Reduce the heat to low and simmer, covered, 15 to 20 minutes.

3. Add the shrimp to the pot and cook until heated through, about 3 to 4 minutes. Taste and adjust the seasonings, if necessary. Remove the bay leaf and discard; serve hot.

✪ Marinated Vegetable Stir-Fry

MAKES 4 SERVINGS

Marinating the vegetables produces deep flavor in this main dish stir-fry. Serve it over brown rice or quinoa for a heartier dish. You can use your favorite vegetables instead, if you wish, cut into even pieces.

3 tablespoons olive oil
¼ cup balsamic vinegar
I teaspoon coarsely chopped fresh oregano or ½ teaspoon dried
I garlic clove, minced
½ teaspoon ground coriander
¼ teaspoon ground cumin
¼ teaspoon salt
¼ teaspoon freshly ground black pepper
2 teaspoons molasses (not blackstrap)
I large onion, cut into ¼-inch slices
4 medium carrots, cut into ¼-inch slices
2 medium zucchini squash, cut into ¼-inch slices
2 small yellow summer squash, cut into ¼-inch slices
I large red bell pepper, cut into ¼-inch slices
I large yellow bell pepper, cut into ¼-inch slices

1. In a large bowl, combine I tablespoon oil, the vinegar, oregano, garlic, coriander, cumin, salt, black pepper, and molasses. Add all the vegetables and let stand 30 minutes. Drain the vegetables and reserve the marinade.

2. In a wok or large, deep skillet, heat the remaining 2 tablespoons oil. Cook the onion and carrots, stirring constantly, until they are crisp-tender, about 5 to 7 minutes. Add the zucchini and yellow squash and cook, stirring constantly, another 2 minutes. Add the bell peppers and cook another minute, stirring constantly.

3. Add 2 to 3 tablespoons of the reserved marinade to the vegetables and cook, stirring constantly, until the vegetables and marinade are hot, about I minute more. Serve immediately.

Vegetable Tempura with Dipping Sauce

MAKES 4 SERVINGS

White rice flour gives this batter a nice crunchiness. This dish is great to serve at a party or slow dinner where everybody gathers around the cook and eats the fried vegetables as soon as they're done.

DIPPING SAUCE
½ cup wheat-free tamari soy sauce
2 tablespoons rice wine vinegar
2 teaspoons honey
Juice of 1 lemon

BATTER
1½ cups white rice flour
¼ cup cornstarch
1 cup cold sparkling mineral water
1 egg yolk, cold
Peanut oil, for frying

VEGETABLES
1 zucchini, cut lengthwise into thin strips
6 thin asparagus stalks, trimmed
1 cup broccoli florets
2 medium carrots, sliced diagonally into thin strips
1 small Japanese eggplant, halved and cut into ¼-inch slices
1 medium sweet potato, peeled and cut into ¼-inch slices
2 large portobello mushrooms, thinly sliced
1 red bell pepper, cut into ½-inch strips
Salt

1. Make the dipping sauce: In a small bowl, whisk together the soy sauce, vinegar, honey, and lemon juice. Set aside.

2. Make the batter: In a medium bowl, whisk together 1 cup rice flour and the cornstarch. Whisk in the sparkling water until the batter is smooth. Add the egg yolk and whisk until the batter is the consistency of heavy cream.

3. Heat 2 to 3 inches oil to 375°F in a wok or deep fryer, according to the manufacturer's directions.

4. Make sure vegetables are dry and dust with ½ cup rice flour; shake off excess. Dip the vegetables into the batter and add 4 pieces of the same vegetable at a time to the hot oil. Fry the vegetables until golden brown, turning once, about 3 minutes. Between batches, skim off the small bits of batter that float in the oil. Drain the vegetables on paper towels; season them with salt to taste. Serve immediately with the dipping sauce.

✪ Chiles Rellenos

MAKES 4 SERVINGS

Chiles rellenos are simply cheese-stuffed peppers that are breaded and fried. You can use your favorite green chile sauce instead of the red chile sauce, if you prefer. Wear gloves while peeling the peppers to protect your hands from the volatile oils.

8 medium poblano peppers
16 thin slices Monterey Jack cheese or cheese alternative (about 4 ounces)
¼ cup cornstarch or white rice flour
4 large eggs, separated and at room temperature
½ teaspoon salt
⅛ teaspoon cream of tartar
¼ cup canola oil
1½ cups gluten-free red chile sauce
½ cup sour cream or sour cream alternative, for garnish (optional)

1. Preheat the broiler. Line a 15 × 10-inch baking sheet with aluminum foil. Arrange the chiles on the sheet and place 6 inches from the broiler. Broil until the skin is blackened on the top side, about 5 to 10 minutes. Turn the chiles over and broil until the other side is blackened and blistered, 5 to 10 minutes more. Remove from the oven and seal in a heavy-duty food storage bag to soften; cool 10 minutes.

2. Peel all the blackened skin from the chiles, using a paper towel to strip the blackened skin away. Try to keep the whole chile intact.

3. With a small paring knife, cut a slit down the long side of the chile. Remove as much of the membrane and seeds as possible, taking care not to tear the chile. Place 2 slices of cheese in each chile, sealing the slit with a toothpick to hold the edges together. Dust the chiles lightly with cornstarch on all sides.

4. In a medium bowl, beat the egg whites, salt, and cream of tartar with an electric mixer on medium-high speed until stiff peaks form. In a small bowl, whisk the egg yolks together and then gently fold them into the egg whites.

5. Heat the oil in a large nonstick (gray, not black) skillet over medium-high heat. Dip 1 chile into the egg mixture and then into the hot oil. Repeat with the second chile and fry the 2 chiles, turning to brown the chiles on all sides, 4 to 5 minutes. Repeat with another 2 chiles. Keep the fried chiles warm in a 200°F oven. Transfer the fried chiles to a serving platter and serve with the chile sauce and sour cream, if using.

DESSERTS

COOKIES AND BARS
Holiday Cut-Out Cookies
Decadent Chocolate Cookies
Ice Cream Cones
Gingersnaps
Chocolate Brownies

CUPCAKES AND CAKES
Yellow Cupcakes
Flourless Dark Chocolate Cake
Devil's Food Layer Cake with Fudge Frosting
Carrot Layer Cake with Cream Cheese Frosting
Basic Butter Cake
Buttermilk Crumb Coffee Cake
New York–Style Cheesecake

PIES, PASTRIES, AND FRUIT DESSERTS
Basic Pastry Crust
Rustic Nectarine Frangipane Tart
Individual Fruit Tarts in Coconut Crusts
Apple Galette
Cherry Pie
Strawberry Pie with Whipped Cream
Frozen Margarita Pie
Cherry Cobbler
Apple Crisp
Chocolate Fudge Espresso Pie
Cannoli
Tiramisù

Holiday Cut-Out Cookies

MAKES 24 COOKIES

This recipe makes a thin, crisp cookie, suitable for cut-out shapes that kids can decorate or frost. You can also use different extracts such as anise, lemon, or peppermint to suit your tastes. If you prefer a plumper cookie, bake them at 375°F just until the edges start to brown.

2¼ cups Carol's Sorghum Blend (page 14)
1 teaspoon xanthan gum
½ teaspoon baking powder
½ teaspoon salt
½ cup (1 stick) unsalted butter or buttery spread, at room
   temperature and cut into tablespoons
1 cup granulated sugar
1 tablespoon packed light brown sugar
1 large egg
1 teaspoon pure vanilla extract
1 teaspoon almond extract
White rice flour, for dusting

1. In a large bowl, whisk together the sorghum blend, xanthan gum, baking powder, and salt. With an electric mixer on low speed, beat in the butter until smooth. Beat in the granulated sugar, brown sugar, egg, vanilla, and almond extract until well blended. Remove the dough from the bowl and knead it with your hands until it is very smooth. Divide the dough in half and pat each half into a flat 1-inch disk. Wrap each disk tightly in plastic wrap and refrigerate for 1 hour.

2. Place a rack in the middle of the oven. Preheat the oven to 375°F. Line a 15 × 10-inch baking sheet (not nonstick) with parchment paper and set aside.

3. Put half of the chilled dough on a 15-inch square piece of parchment paper that is dusted with white rice flour. Cut a piece of plastic wrap the same size as the parchment paper, lay it on top of the dough, sprinkle it with white rice flour, and roll the dough with a rolling pin to ¼-inch thickness. Remove the plastic wrap and cut the dough into desired shapes, reserving the scraps. Arrange the cookies 1 inch apart on the prepared baking sheet. Cut the second half of the dough into shapes. Reroll the scraps from both halves, cut more cookies, and arrange on the baking sheet. If your baking sheet won't hold all of the cookies, bake in two batches.

4. Bake the cookies, rotating the sheet halfway through baking, until the edges are golden brown, 10 to 15 minutes. Cool the cookies on the baking sheet on a wire rack for 2 minutes. Remove the cookies from the baking sheet and cool completely on the wire rack. Bake the second half of the cookies and cool in the same manner. Store undecorated cookies, tightly covered, for up to 2 days or in the freezer for up to 1 month.

5. Decorate as desired with frosting, sprinkles, coconut, raisins, gluten-free chocolate chips, and so on.

TIPS FOR MAKING CUT-OUT COOKIES

• For best results, use a light-colored cookie sheet rather than gray or black nonstick types. Line the sheet with parchment paper or use baking liners (such as Silpat) to help reduce excessive browning. Insulated baking sheets assure even baking and won't buckle.

• Metal cookie cutters work better than plastic cookie cutters because they make sharper cuts. Do not roll the dough thinner than ¼ inch.

• If the chilled dough is too stiff, leave the dough at room temperature 15 to 20 minutes. Or knead it with your hands to make the dough more pliable. If the dough is too soft after rolling, chill it until firm, then cut into desired shapes. Chill shaped cookies 30 minutes before baking if the dough is still too soft.

• If you're having trouble transferring the cookies to the baking sheet, try rolling the dough onto parchment paper or a nonstick liner, cut desired shapes, remove scraps of dough (leaving cut-out cookies on the paper or liner), and transfer the paper or liner (cookies and all) to the baking sheet.

✿ Decadent Chocolate Cookies

MAKES 48 COOKIES

Chocoholics will adore this cookie! Mostly chocolate, sugar, eggs, and nuts—with only a little flour for stability—the deep, rich chocolate flavor really shines through. For variation, replace the cranberries with chopped candied ginger or dried cherries. White chocolate chips can replace the chocolate chips.

9 ounces gluten-free bittersweet chocolate (at least 60 percent cocoa)
5 tablespoons unsalted butter or buttery spread
3 large eggs
1 cup sugar
½ teaspoon pure vanilla extract
½ cup sorghum flour
¼ teaspoon baking soda
¼ teaspoon xanthan gum
¼ teaspoon salt
1 cup finely chopped walnuts
½ cup dried cranberries
1 (12-ounce) bag gluten-free semisweet chocolate chips

1. In a medium microwave-safe bowl, heat the chocolate and butter in the microwave on low until melted, 1 to 2 minutes. Stir until well blended; set aside.

2. In a large bowl, beat the eggs, sugar, and vanilla with an electric mixer on low speed until thick, about 1 minute. In a small bowl, whisk together the sorghum flour, baking soda, xanthan gum, and salt and beat into the eggs on low speed until no flour streaks remain. Beat in the melted chocolate mixture. Stir in the walnuts, cranberries, and chocolate chips. The dough will be very soft. Cover the bowl tightly and refrigerate for 2 hours.

3. Place an oven rack in the middle position of the oven. Preheat the oven to 375°F. Line a 15 × 10-inch baking sheet (not nonstick) with parchment paper.

4. Shape the dough into 48 walnut-size balls with your hands and place 12 balls 1½ inches apart on the sheet. Keep the remaining balls of dough chilled.

5. Bake just until the cookies look shiny and the crust starts to crack, 10 to 12 minutes. Cool the cookies 2 minutes on the pan; then transfer to a wire rack to cool completely. Repeat with the remaining balls of chilled dough, 12 per sheet. Store, tightly covered, for up to 2 days or in the freezer for up to 1 month.

Ice Cream Cones

 MAKES 36 CONES

Your kitchen will smell like an old-fashioned ice cream shop when you make these waffle-style cones. Make small ones with an electric pizzelle iron or large ones with an electric waffle cone maker; both are found in kitchen stores or online. These cones are best when made with real butter or Fleischmann's margarine.

1¾ cups Carol's Sorghum Blend (page 14)
2 teaspoons baking powder
½ teaspoon xanthan gum
⅛ teaspoon salt
3 large eggs
¾ cup sugar
¼ cup (½ stick) unsalted butter or Fleischmann's margarine, melted
1 teaspoon pure vanilla extract, or to taste
Ice cream, sherbet, frozen yogurt, or sorbet of choice

1. In a small bowl, sift together the sorghum blend, baking powder, xanthan gum, and salt; set aside.

2. In a medium bowl, beat the eggs and sugar with an electric mixer on medium speed until thick and pale yellow, about 30 seconds. On low speed, beat in the butter and vanilla and then gradually beat in the flour mixture until the batter is smooth, about 1 minute.

3. Heat the pizzelle iron or waffle cone maker and brush with oil, if necessary. Drop 1 tablespoon batter onto each circle of the pizzelle iron for a small cone or 3 tablespoons onto the waffle cone maker for a larger cone. Gently lower the lid but do not press it shut.

4. Bake following the manufacturer's directions, or until steam no longer comes out of the iron. Baking times will vary by machine; small cones take 10 to 15 seconds in a pizzelle iron, compared to 60 seconds in the larger waffle cone maker. Often, the first one or two cones will not turn out well; simply discard them. The oil in the batter will season the iron for successive cones, but brush the iron with oil to prevent sticking, if necessary.

5. Use the tines of a fork to carefully remove the cookies from the iron and wrap around the cone provided with the waffle cone maker or shape by hand into a cone, sealing the bottom shut with your fingers. (Wear rubber gloves if the cones are too hot to handle.) Stand the cone upright in a drinking glass to cool. They will harden further as they cool. Store, tightly covered, for up to 2 days or in the freezer for up to 1 month. Fill with your choice of frozen treat and serve.

 # Gingersnaps

MAKES 24 COOKIES

Gingersnaps are wonderful for traveling, for dipping in coffee, and as cookie crumb crusts for pies. Their delicious flavor and intoxicating aroma are perfect at any holiday festivity.

½ cup (1 stick) unsalted butter or buttery spread, at room temperature
1 cup packed light brown sugar
1 large egg
3 tablespoons molasses (not blackstrap)
1 teaspoon pure vanilla extract
1 teaspoon almond extract
2½ cups Carol's Sorghum Blend (page 14)
1 teaspoon xanthan gum
1½ teaspoons ground ginger
1½ teaspoons ground cinnamon
½ teaspoon baking powder
½ teaspoon salt
¼ teaspoon freshly grated nutmeg
¼ teaspoon ground cloves
2 tablespoons granulated sugar, for rolling

1. Place a rack in the lower-middle position and another in the upper-middle position of the oven. Preheat the oven to 375°F. Line two 15 × 10-inch baking sheets (not nonstick) with parchment paper.

2. In a large bowl, beat the butter and brown sugar with an electric mixer on low speed until smooth, about 30 seconds. Beat in the egg, molasses, vanilla, and almond extract. Gradually add the sorghum blend, xanthan gum, ginger, cinnamon, baking powder, salt, nutmeg, and cloves and beat on low speed just until blended.

3. With wet hands or a #50 metal ice cream scoop, shape the dough into 1½-inch balls, roll them in the granulated sugar, and place them 2 inches apart on the baking sheets, 12 per sheet. Sprinkle the cookies with any remaining granulated sugar. Place one sheet on the lower-middle rack and another on the upper-middle rack of the oven.

4. Bake until firm, switching the baking sheets halfway through baking, 15 to 20 minutes. Cool the cookies 2 to 3 minutes on the baking sheet, then transfer them to a wire rack to cool completely. Store, tightly covered, for up to 2 days or in the freezer for up to 1 month.

Chocolate Brownies

This basic brownie recipe is fabulous and decadent, but also try the Rocky Road Brownie variation for the kids. (If you use coffee, use decaf when serving kids.)

3 ounces gluten-free semisweet baking chocolate, melted
⅓ cup unsalted butter or buttery spread, melted, or canola oil
¾ cup packed light brown sugar
2 large eggs, at room temperature
1 teaspoon pure vanilla extract
1 cup Carol's Sorghum Blend (page 14)
½ cup unsweetened cocoa powder (not Dutch-process)
1 teaspoon xanthan gum
½ teaspoon baking powder
½ teaspoon salt
¼ cup hot water or freshly brewed hot coffee (about 120°F)
¼ cup coarsely chopped walnuts

1. Place a rack in the middle of the oven. Preheat the oven to 350°F. Generously grease an 8-inch square glass baking dish.

2. In a medium bowl, combine the chocolate with the butter and brown sugar and beat with an electric mixer on low speed until smooth, about 30 seconds. Beat in the eggs and vanilla until thoroughly blended. Add the sorghum blend, cocoa, xanthan gum, baking powder, and salt and beat until thoroughly blended, about 30 seconds. Blend in the hot water. Stir in the walnuts. Transfer the batter to the prepared pan and smooth the top with a wet rubber spatula.

3. Bake 20 minutes. Don't overbake. Remove from the oven and cool on a wire rack for 20 minutes. The brownies will firm up as they cool. Cut into 16 squares and serve at room temperature. Store leftovers at room temperature, tightly covered, for up to 1 day.

ROCKY ROAD BROWNIES

In step 3, bake the brownies 15 minutes. Sprinkle 1 cup miniature marshmallows, ½ cup chopped pecans, and ½ cup gluten-free semisweet chocolate chips on top of the partially baked brownies. Bake until the marshmallows and chips melt slightly, about 5 minutes more. Remove from the oven and cool completely on a wire rack before cutting into squares.

Yellow Cupcakes

 MAKES 12 CUPCAKES

Simple yellow cupcakes are incredibly versatile. See the sidebar on page 158 for decorating ideas. For a small layer cake, bake the batter in two 8-inch nonstick cake pans, parchment lined and generously greased, for 20 to 25 minutes.

½ cup (1 stick) unsalted butter or buttery spread, at room
    temperature, or ⅓ cup canola oil
1 cup sugar
2 large eggs, at room temperature
1¾ cups Carol's Sorghum Blend (page 14)
1½ teaspoons baking powder
1 teaspoon xanthan gum
½ teaspoon salt
1 cup milk of choice
1 teaspoon pure vanilla extract
½ teaspoon almond extract

1. Place a rack in the middle of the oven. Preheat the oven to 325°F. Generously grease each cup of a standard 12-cup nonstick (gray, not black) muffin pan or line with paper liners.

2. In a large bowl, beat the butter with an electric mixer on medium speed until smooth, about 30 seconds. Gradually beat in the sugar until smooth, about 30 seconds. Add the eggs, 1 at a time, beating well after each addition.

3. In a medium bowl, sift together the sorghum blend, baking powder, xanthan gum, and salt. In a measuring cup, whisk together the milk, vanilla, and almond extract.

4. With the mixer on low speed, alternately beat the sorghum mixture and milk mixture into the butter-egg mixture. Divide the batter evenly in the muffin pan.

5. Bake until a toothpick inserted into the center of a cupcake comes out clean, 25 to 30 minutes. Cool the cupcakes in the pan 5 minutes and then transfer them to a wire rack to cool completely. Serve plain or with your favorite frosting.

CREAM-FILLED CAKES

CREAM FILLING
1 (7-ounce) jar marshmallow cream
¼ cup white shortening, at room temperature
3 tablespoons powdered sugar
¼ teaspoon pure vanilla extract

1. Prepare the cupcake batter through step 4, above, but bake in a generously greased canoe cake pan or a cream twinkle pan at 325°F for 20 to 25 minutes, or until the tops of the cakes are golden brown and a toothpick inserted into the center comes out clean.

2. Cool the cakes in the pan on a wire rack for 5 minutes. Remove the cakes from the pans with a thin metal spatula and cool completely on the wire rack.

3. Make the cream filling: In a medium bowl, beat the marsh-mallow cream and shortening together with an electric mixer on medium speed until well blended. Beat in the sugar and vanilla until smooth. Transfer the filling to a gallon-size, heavy-duty freezer storage bag or a pastry bag fitted with a plastic tip.

4. Poke holes in 3 to 4 places down the center of the cake's flat side (the top as it bakes). Place the tip into the flat side of the cake and squirt a little of the filling into the holes. Be careful not to squirt too much or too hard or it will break the cake. Serve at room temperature.

CUPCAKES FOR EVERY OCCASION

Vary the cupcakes by mixing in grated orange or lemon zest or topping them with vanilla or chocolate frosting. Decorate with fresh fruit, chocolate shavings, candied fruit, cocoa nibs, chocolate-covered espresso beans, or nuts. Sliced in half horizontally and layered with sliced strawberries and whipped cream, cupcakes make perfect strawberry shortcakes.

 Flourless Dark Chocolate Cake

MAKES 10 SERVINGS

Hershey's Special Dark cocoa, available in grocery stores, works especially well in this recipe and dissolving it in hot water enhances its flavor. This is a very dark cake—perfect for special occasions because it looks so rich and decadent.

½ cup Hershey's Special Dark cocoa powder
½ cup boiling water
2 cups whole almonds
¾ cup packed light brown sugar
3 large eggs, at room temperature
⅓ cup unsalted butter or buttery spread, melted, or canola oil
1 tablespoon pure vanilla extract
½ teaspoon salt
2 tablespoons powdered sugar, for dusting

1. Place a rack in the middle of the oven. Preheat the oven to 350°F. Generously grease and then line the bottom of an 8-inch springform pan with parchment or wax paper. Grease again; set aside.

2. In a small bowl, dissolve the cocoa in the water; set aside. Meanwhile, grind the nuts in a food processor to a fine meal.

3. Add the cocoa-water mixture, sugar, eggs, butter, vanilla, and salt to the food processor and process 30 to 40 seconds. Scrape down the sides of the bowl with a rubber spatula and process until the mixture is thoroughly blended, about another 30 seconds. Spread the batter evenly in the prepared pan.

4. Bake until a toothpick inserted into the center of the cake comes out clean, 40 to 45 minutes. (The cake rises as it bakes, then falls slightly as it cools.) Cool the cake in the pan on a wire rack for 10 minutes. Gently run a sharp knife around the edge of the pan to loosen the cake. Release the pan sides; discard the paper liner. Dust with powdered sugar before serving.

✿ Devil's Food Layer Cake with Fudge Frosting

MAKES 8 SERVINGS

Devilishly good, this recipe makes a chic little layer cake that's perfect for small families or dinner parties.

CAKE

- 1½ cups Carol's Sorghum Blend (page 14)
- 1 cup granulated sugar
- ½ cup unsweetened cocoa powder (not Dutch-process)
- ¾ teaspoon baking soda
- 1 teaspoon xanthan gum
- ¾ teaspoon salt
- 1 cup buttermilk (thinned with ¼ cup water if thick) or Homemade Buttermilk (page 29), well shaken
- 1 tablespoon pure vanilla extract
- ½ cup (1 stick) unsalted butter or buttery spread, at room temperature, or ⅓ cup canola oil
- 2 large eggs, at room temperature

FROSTING

- ½ cup (1 stick) unsalted butter or buttery spread, or ⅓ cup canola oil
- ⅓ cup milk of choice
- 3½ cups powdered sugar
- ¼ cup natural or Dutch-process unsweetened cocoa powder
- ⅛ teaspoon salt
- 1 tablespoon pure vanilla extract
- ¼ cup chopped walnuts

1. Place a rack in the middle of the oven. Preheat the oven to 350°F. Generously grease two 8-inch round nonstick (gray, not black) cake pans. Line with parchment or wax paper and grease again; set aside.

2. Make the cake: In a medium bowl, sift together the sorghum blend, sugar, cocoa, baking soda, xanthan gum, and salt; set aside. In a measuring cup, combine the buttermilk and vanilla extract; set aside.

3. In a large bowl, beat the butter with an electric mixer on low speed, scraping down the side of the bowl with a rubber spatula, for 1 minute. Add the eggs, one at a time, beating thoroughly after each addition.

4. With the mixer on low speed, add the sorghum mixture alternately with the buttermilk mixture, beginning and ending with the sorghum mixture. Spread the batter evenly in the prepared pans.

5. Bake until the cakes start to pull away from the edges of the pan and a toothpick inserted into the center of the cakes comes out clean, 25 to 30 minutes. Cool in the pans on a wire rack for 10 minutes. Remove the cakes from the pans with a thin metal spatula, discard the paper, and cool completely on a wire rack.

6. Make the frosting: In a medium saucepan, combine the butter and milk and cook over medium heat until the butter is melted. Add the powdered sugar, cocoa, and salt and bring to a boil over high heat. Remove from the heat and transfer the mixture to a medium bowl. Beat the mixture with an electric mixer on medium speed until the frosting reaches the consistency of thin fudge. Stir in the vanilla extract; use immediately.

7. To frost the cake, place one cake layer, top-side down, on a serving platter. Spread one-quarter of the frosting on top and out to the edges. Place the remaining layer on top of the frosting, top-side up. Spread one-quarter of the frosting on top. Spread the remaining frosting on the sides of the cake. Sprinkle with nuts. Serve immediately.

CHOCOLATE CUPCAKES

In step 4, divide the batter evenly in a standard 12-cup muffin pan that is generously greased or lined with paper liners. Bake at 325°F for 20 to 25 minutes. Cool the cupcakes in the pan for 5 minutes and then place them on a wire rack to finish cooling completely. Serve plain or with your favorite frosting.

✺ Carrot Layer Cake with Cream Cheese Frosting

MAKES 12 SERVINGS

Fragrant and moist, this cake is perfect at any occasion—even weddings (it perfectly fills a 15 × 10-inch half sheet pan). It is a large cake, so you will need three 9-inch round cake pans if you make a layer cake.

CAKE
  3 cups Carol's Sorghum Blend (page 14)
  1½ teaspoons xanthan gum
  1 teaspoon baking soda
  2 teaspoons pumpkin pie spice
  1 teaspoon ground ginger
  ¾ teaspoon salt
  4 large eggs, at room temperature
  1 cup granulated sugar
  ¾ cup packed light brown sugar
  ½ cup (1 stick) unsalted butter or buttery spread, at room temperature, or ⅓ cup canola oil
  ¾ cup buttermilk or Homemade Buttermilk (page 29), well shaken
  1 teaspoon pure vanilla extract
  2 cups finely shredded carrots
  1 (8-ounce) can crushed pineapple, drained
  ¾ cup sweetened shredded coconut
  ⅓ cup finely chopped walnuts

FROSTING
  1 (8-ounce) package cream cheese or cream cheese alternative, at room temperature
  2 tablespoons milk of choice or pineapple juice
  1 teaspoon pure vanilla extract
  3 cups powdered sugar
  ¼ cup sweetened shredded coconut (toasted, optional)
  ⅛ teaspoon salt
  1 cup sweetened shredded coconut, toasted, for garnish

1. Place a rack in the middle of the oven. Preheat the oven to 325°F. Generously grease three round 9-inch nonstick (gray, not black) cake pans. Line the bottom of the pans with parchment or wax paper and grease again; set aside.

2. Make the cakes: In a medium bowl, sift the sorghum blend, xanthan gum, baking soda, pumpkin pie spice, ginger, and salt; set aside.

(continued on following page)

3. In a large bowl, beat the eggs, both sugars, butter, buttermilk, and vanilla with an electric mixer on medium speed until smooth. Add the sorghum mixture slowly on low speed, then increase the speed to medium and beat until smooth, about 30 seconds. With a large rubber spatula, fold in the carrots, pineapple, coconut, and walnuts. Divide the batter evenly among the prepared pans.

4. Bake until the cakes pull away from the sides of the pans and a toothpick inserted in the center of the cakes comes out clean, 40 to 45 minutes. Cool the cakes on a wire rack for 15 minutes. Remove the cakes from the pans with a thin metal spatula, discard the paper liner, and cool completely on the wire rack.

5. Make the frosting: In a medium bowl, beat the cream cheese, milk, and vanilla with an electric mixer on medium speed until very smooth. With the mixer on low speed, gradually beat in the sugar until the frosting is smooth. Stir in the shredded coconut and salt.

6. Place one cake layer, top-side down, on a serving plate. Spread one-fourth of the frosting on top. Place the second layer on top, and spread another fourth of the frosting over the top. Add the third cake layer and top with the remaining frosting, spreading it evenly on the top and sides. Sprinkle with the toasted coconut. Serve immediately. Refrigerate leftovers, covered, for up to 1 day.

☀ Basic Butter Cake

MAKES 10 SERVINGS

This simple, moist cake has its origins in the classic French butter sponge cake called genoise (jen-WAHZ). It is leavened by beating air into eggs. Quite versatile, it can be served plain or dressed up in a variety of ways with frosting, whipped cream, fruit sauces, or a simple dusting of powdered sugar.

I cup potato starch, plus extra for dusting pan
2 tablespoons plus ½ cup sugar
⅛ teaspoon salt
⅛ teaspoon xanthan gum
4 large eggs
2 teaspoons pure vanilla extract
2 tablespoons unsalted butter or buttery spread, melted

1. Place a rack in the middle of the oven. Preheat the oven to 350°F. Generously grease a 10-inch cake pan and line the bottom with parchment paper. Grease again and dust the bottom and sides with potato starch; set aside.

2. Over a sheet of wax paper, sift together the I cup potato starch, 2 tablespoons sugar, salt, and xanthan gum three times; set aside.

3. Place the eggs in the large bowl of a heavy-duty stand mixer and place the bowl over a pot of simmering, not boiling, water (the bowl should not touch the water). Whisk the sugar into the eggs and continue to whisk until the mixture is body temperature when tested with your finger.

4. Transfer the bowl to the stand mixer and beat the mixture on medium-high speed until it becomes pale yellow in color and falls off the beater in long ribbons, 7 to 8 minutes. Beat in the vanilla.

5. Sift about one-third of the flour mixture into the eggs and gently fold in with a rubber spatula until no flour streaks remain. Continue to fold in the flour mixture, one-third at a time. Gently fold in the butter. Pour the batter into the prepared pan.

6. Bake until the top is light brown and a toothpick inserted into the center comes out clean, 30 to 35 minutes. Cool the cake in the pan on a wire rack for 10 to 15 minutes. Run a sharp knife around the edge of the pan to loosen the cake and then invert it onto a plate. Then invert it onto a cake stand or serving plate, top-side up. Cool completely before frosting.

✱ Buttermilk Crumb Coffee Cake

MAKES 10 SERVINGS

This delicious coffee cake is rich and satisfying and makes a great brunch dish. You can also add ¼ cup of finely chopped nuts such as walnuts or pecans to the topping for added crunch.

CAKE

5 tablespoons unsalted butter or buttery spread, at room temperature
1 cup firmly packed light brown sugar
1 large egg, at room temperature
1 cup buttermilk or Homemade Buttermilk (page 29), well shaken
2 teaspoons pure vanilla extract
1½ cups Carol's Sorghum Blend (page 14)
1½ teaspoons xanthan gum
1 teaspoon ground cinnamon
¾ teaspoon baking soda
¾ teaspoon salt

TOPPING

¼ cup Carol's Sorghum Blend (page 14)
¼ cup firmly packed light brown sugar
2 tablespoons unsalted butter or buttery spread, at room temperature

1. Place a rack in the middle of the oven. Preheat the oven to 350°F. Generously grease an 11 × 7-inch nonstick (gray, not black) rectangular pan.

2. Make the cake: In a large bowl, beat the butter and sugar with an electric mixer on medium speed until light and fluffy, about 30 seconds. Beat in the egg on medium speed until smooth. In a measuring cup, whisk together the buttermilk and vanilla.

3. In a small bowl, whisk together the sorghum blend, xanthan gum, cinnamon, baking soda, and salt. With the mixer on low speed, beat the sorghum mixture into the egg mixture, alternating with the buttermilk mixture, beginning and ending with the sorghum mixture. Beat until the batter is smooth and thickens slightly, about 30 seconds. Spread the batter evenly in the prepared pan.

4. Make the topping: In a small bowl, combine the sorghum blend and sugar. Cut in the butter with a fork until the mixture resembles coarse crumbs. Sprinkle on top of the cake batter.

5. Bake the cake until the top of the cake is golden brown and a toothpick inserted into the center comes out clean, about 35 minutes. Cool the cake in the pan on a wire rack for 10 minutes. Serve warm.

✦ New York–Style Cheesecake
MAKES 12 SERVINGS

This is the quintessential cheesecake. Serve it plain
or topped with fruit, such as strawberries or blueberries. Or vary the flavor by adding 2 tablespoons of your
favorite liqueur such as amaretto, Cointreau, or Kahlúa
to the filling.

CRUST
9 gluten-free vanilla or lemon cookies
1 tablespoon sugar
2 tablespoons unsalted butter or buttery spread, melted, or canola oil

FILLING
3 (8-ounce) packages cream cheese or cream cheese alternative,
   cut into 1-inch cubes and softened
1 cup sugar
¼ cup sour cream or sour cream alternative, at room temperature
Juice and grated zest of 1 lemon
1½ teaspoons pure vanilla extract
⅛ teaspoon salt
3 large eggs, at room temperature

1. Place a rack in the middle of the oven. Preheat the oven to
325°F. Generously grease the bottom and sides of a 9-inch nonstick (gray, not black) springform pan; set aside.

2. Make the crust: Place the cookies and sugar in a food processor and process until they are fine crumbs. Add the butter and
process until the mixture is crumbly. Pat the crust into the bottom
of the pan. Bake 10 to 12 minutes, or just until the crust is fragrant.
Cool the crust while preparing the filling, but leave the oven on.

3. Make the filling: In a large bowl, beat the cream cheese with an
electric mixer on medium speed until light and fluffy. Add the sugar
and sour cream and beat 1 minute, scraping down the side of the bowl
with a rubber spatula. Add the lemon juice and zest, vanilla, and salt
and beat until smooth. Beat in the eggs, one a time, just until blended.
Pour the filling over the crust and smooth with a wet rubber spatula.

4. Bake until the top is firm, about 1 hour. Cool the cheesecake
on a wire rack for 15 minutes. Run a sharp knife around the outer
edge of the cake to loosen the edges and remove the sides of the
pan. Wrap the cheesecake in plastic and refrigerate overnight. Slide
a thin metal knife between the cheesecake and the pan and slide
the cheesecake onto a serving plate. Let stand at room temperature. Cut with a knife dipped in hot water, then dried. Refrigerate
leftovers, covered, for up to 1 day.

✳ Basic Pastry Crust

MAKES ONE 9-INCH DOUBLE-CRUST PIECRUST OR TWO 9-INCH SINGLE-CRUST PIECRUSTS

Use this basic piecrust in any type of pie that calls for a pastry crust. If you only need enough pie dough for a single-crust pie, make the whole recipe and freeze the remaining half of dough tightly wrapped, for another pie up to two months later. This piecrust is also suitable for savory piecrusts such as quiches.

I cup Carol's Sorghum Blend (page 14)
¾ cup tapioca flour
½ cup sweet rice flour
3 tablespoons sugar
I teaspoon xanthan gum
I teaspoon guar gum
½ teaspoon salt
⅛ teaspoon baking soda
½ cup shortening or buttery spread
½ cup milk of choice
I teaspoon vinegar or fresh lemon juice
I egg white beaten with I tablespoon water, for egg wash (optional)

1. In a food processor, place the sorghum blend, tapioca flour, rice flour, 2 tablespoons sugar, xanthan gum, guar gum, salt, baking soda, and shortening and process until crumbly. Add the milk and vinegar and process until the dough forms a ball. If it doesn't form a ball, use a rubber spatula to break up the dough into pieces and process again, scraping down the sides, if necessary. Remove the dough from the food processor and knead with your hands until smooth. Shape the dough into two 1-inch-thick disks, wrap tightly with plastic wrap, and refrigerate for 1 hour.

2. For single-crust pie: Massage 1 disk of the dough between your hands until it is pliable and feels as warm as your hands, making the crust easier to handle. With a rolling pin, roll the dough to a 10-inch circle between two pieces of heavy-duty plastic wrap dusted with rice flour. (Use a damp paper towel between the countertop and plastic wrap to anchor the plastic.) Roll the rolling pin from the center of the dough to the outer edge, moving around the circle in clockwise fashion to assure a uniform thickness.

3. Remove the top plastic wrap and invert the crust, centering it over a 9-inch nonstick (gray, not black) pie pan. Press the dough into place before removing the remaining plastic. Trim the edges to an even overhang around the edge of the pan. Shape a decorative edge if you are making a single-crust pie. If not, leave the overhang in place.

4. For double-crust pie: Follow steps 1, 2, and 3 above. Add the filling as directed per your recipe. Roll the remaining disk of dough to a 10-inch circle, invert, and center on the filled crust. Do not remove the top plastic wrap until the dough is centered. Trim the top crust to the same overhang as the bottom crust. Press the two crusts together and shape a decorative edge around the rim of the pan. Freeze 15 minutes. Brush with the beaten egg and sprinkle with the remaining tablespoon of sugar. Prick the top crust several times with a fork to allow the steam to escape. Place the pan on a nonstick baking sheet and bake per your recipe's instructions.

KIDS' PASTRY TREATS

Thinly roll leftover scraps of pie dough on a parchment paper–lined baking sheet, lightly sprinkle with equal parts ground cinnamon and sugar, and bake at 375°F until lightly browned around the edges, about 5 to 10 minutes.

GLUTEN-FREE PIECRUST TIPS

Put two freshly baked cherry pies side by side—one gluten-free, the other not—and you'd be hard-pressed to tell which was which. Both are delicious, but each was assembled quite differently. Once you make a few pies in this new manner, it will seem quite easy and familiar. Remember, practice makes perfect—the more pies you make, the more skillful you'll become. And your family will love it.

Compared to piecrust made from wheat flour, gluten-free piecrust:

• Looks the same at the dough stage, but uses a variety of flours (instead of one single flour), plus xanthan and guar gums for cohesiveness.

• Is rolled and shaped while it is warm rather than cool—preferably as warm as your hands for maximum ease of handling. If gluten-free piecrust is rolled when cold, it will be very crumbly and difficult to handle. If you chill the dough, massage and knead it with your hands until it feels the same temperature as your hands.

• Is more delicate and tears more easily, so roll the dough between sheets of heavy-duty plastic wrap to minimize tears and make it easier to transfer the crust to the pie pan. This fragile nature discourages wrapping the dough around a rolling pin. It also makes shaping and fluting the dough a bit more challenging. If a tear occurs, just press the torn edges together to eliminate it or place a scrap of dough over the hole and press it until smooth. The dough is too delicate to weave a lattice top, but you can achieve a lattice look by using a pie top cutter found in kitchen stores.

• Bakes in nonstick (gray, not black) pans (rather than glass or ceramic), which transfer heat to the crust more thoroughly as it bakes and seals it, leading to a crispier crust that doesn't absorb as much liquid from the filling. This reduces the tendency toward sogginess.

• Bakes on the bottom rack of the oven for the first 10 to 15 minutes so it is closer to the source of the heat. This browns the bottom of the piecrust and further reduces the chance of sogginess. Shift the pie to the middle rack for the remainder of the baking time; it will burn if left on the bottom rack.

• Works best with fillings that require a shorter baking time such as peaches, cherries, and blueberries rather than longer-cooking fillings such as apples because the longer baking time causes the crust edges to brown too much and become hard. For longer-cooking filings, cover the crust edges with foil or a piecrust shield, available at kitchen stores.

• Is best eaten on the same day it was baked, at room temperature, rather than straight from the oven. This gives the juices, especially in fruit pies, time to firm up. If you must chill the pie, bring it to room temperature on the countertop before serving. Microwaving gluten-free piecrust can make it soggy.

 Rustic Nectarine Frangipane Tart

MAKES 6 SERVINGS

A frangipane (frahn-gee-PAH-ne) is a fruit-topped almond filling or batter, usually baked in a sweet pastry.
Nectarines don't have to be peeled and their lovely red
skin is especially pretty in this tart. You can use other
stone fruits such as plums or peaches.

Basic Pastry Crust for a 9-inch single-crust pie (page 168)
1 (8-ounce) can gluten-free almond paste
4 firm ripe nectarines, pitted and cut in ¼-inch wedges
1 teaspoon almond extract
¼ teaspoon salt
3 tablespoons sugar
⅓ cup apple jelly, melted
1 tablespoon water

1. Place a rack in the bottom position and another in the middle
position of the oven. Preheat the oven to 375°F. Have a 13 × 9-
inch nonstick (gray, not black) baking sheet ready.

2. Prepare the pastry crust as directed through step 2 on page
168. Remove the top sheet of the plastic wrap and slide the parchment paper (with the piecrust on it) onto the baking sheet.

3. Place the almond paste between two sheets of plastic wrap
and roll it to an 8-inch diameter. Remove 1 sheet of plastic wrap, and
invert the almond paste over the piecrust. Remove the plastic wrap.

4. In a large bowl, toss the nectarines with the almond extract
and salt. Arrange the nectarines in a concentric circle (or pattern
of your choice) on top of the almond paste. Roll or push the edges
of the piecrust toward the center of the pie and crimp or flute
the edges. The piecrust may break or tear; simply press the tears
together. Sprinkle 2 tablespoons of the sugar over the nectarines
and the remaining tablespoon on the piecrust.

5. Bake 15 minutes on the bottom rack of the oven. Move to the
middle rack of the oven and bake until the piecrust is browned and
the nectarines are tender, about 15 minutes more. Remove from
the oven. Combine the apple jelly with the water and brush on the
nectarines and the piecrust. Cool completely on a wire rack before
serving.

✺ Individual Fruit Tarts in Coconut Crusts

MAKES 4 SERVINGS

You can use this dessert to showcase local fruit that is in season, such as the fresh raspberries used here. The coconut crust provides a crunchy contrast to the fruit and is a wonderful alternative to pastry crusts.

CRUST
- 1½ cups sweetened shredded coconut
- 1 tablespoon sweet rice flour
- ¼ teaspoon salt
- 1 teaspoon pure vanilla extract
- 2 tablespoons unsalted butter or buttery spread, melted

FILLING
- ¾ cup whipped topping
- 1 teaspoon almond extract
- ¾ cup mascarpone cheese or cream cheese alternative, softened
- 1 cup fresh raspberries
- ½ cup apple jelly

1. Place a rack in the middle of the oven. Preheat the oven to 325°F. Generously grease 4 nonstick (gray, not black) mini spring-form pans and put them on a baking sheet; set aside.

2. Make the crust: In a large bowl, toss the coconut with the rice flour and salt until blended. Add the vanilla and butter and toss until the coconut is coated. Press the mixture evenly into the 4 pans.

3. Bake until the coconut crust is lightly browned, rotating the baking sheet halfway through baking, about 15 minutes. Remove from the oven and cool completely on a wire rack.

4. Make the filling: In a medium bowl, combine the whipped topping and almond extract. Fold in the mascarpone. Evenly fill the 4 tart shells with the cheese mixture. Arrange the raspberries on top of the cheese mixture.

5. In a small saucepan, melt the jelly and pour evenly over the tarts. Let the tarts stand at room temperature until the jelly firms up before removing the sides of the pans, about 30 minutes. Serve at room temperature.

INDIVIDUAL APRICOT TARTS IN COCONUT CRUSTS

In step 4, replace the raspberries with 2 fresh apricots, halved and pitted, cut-side down, in each tart.

Apple Galette

MAKES 6 SERVINGS

A galette is a free-form pie, rather than one that is fitted into a pie pan. It's okay if the crust breaks or doesn't look perfect; galettes are rustic and casually formed, rather than perfectly shaped.

Basic Pastry Crust for a 9-inch single-crust pie (page 168)
White rice flour, for rolling
2 large apples, peeled, cored, and cut in ⅛-inch slices
½ cup dried cranberries
2 tablespoons sugar
¼ cup coarsely chopped walnuts
¼ teaspoon ground cinnamon
2 tablespoons fresh lemon juice
2 tablespoons corn syrup
1 teaspoon boiling water

1. Place a rack in the middle of the oven. Preheat the oven to 375°F. Have a 13 × 9-inch nonstick (gray, not black) rimmed baking sheet ready.

2. Prepare the single-crust pastry dough as directed through step 2 on page 168. Transfer the parchment paper, with the crust on it, to the baking sheet. Remove the plastic wrap.

3. In a large bowl, toss the apples, cranberries, 1 tablespoon sugar, the walnuts, cinnamon, and lemon juice, and arrange the mixture in the center of the piecrust but no closer than 2 inches from the edge. With a thin metal spatula, lift up the sides of the crust slightly and gently flip it toward the center, covering the filling by about 1 inch. Overlap the crust slightly as you work around the circle of the crust, gently lifting it up and toward the center of the pie. If the crust breaks, simply press it together with your fingers.

4. Bake 20 minutes. Whisk the corn syrup and water together and brush it on the crust. Sprinkle the remaining 1 tablespoon sugar on the crust and over the apple filling. Bake until the crust is golden brown and the apples are tender, 15 to 20 minutes more. Cool the galette on a wire rack for 20 minutes. Serve warm or at room temperature.

Cherry Pie

MAKES 6 SERVINGS

Nothing says summer like cherry pie, especially if you find fresh cherries in season. Since most nonstick pie pans (gray, not black) are "deep-dish size," this pie holds lots of filling. This cherry filling firms up nicely because you first cook it with cornstarch to thicken it before adding it to the piecrust.

I cup sugar plus I tablespoon, for sprinkling on crust
¼ cup cornstarch
⅛ teaspoon salt
4 cups fresh tart red cherries or 3 (14- to 15-ounce) cans cherries, thoroughly drained
I teaspoon almond extract
Basic Pastry Crust for a 9-inch double-crust pie (page 168)
White rice flour, for dusting
2 tablespoons unsalted butter or buttery spread, at room temperature and cut into 6 pieces
I tablespoon heavy cream, apple juice, or beaten egg white, for brushing on crust

1. In a medium, heavy saucepan, whisk together I cup sugar, the cornstarch, and salt until well blended. Add the cherries and cook over medium heat, stirring constantly, until the mixture thickens and becomes clear. Remove from the heat, stir in the almond extract, and set aside to cool.

2. Place a rack in the bottom position and another in the middle position of the oven. Preheat the oven to 375°F. Prepare the double-crust pastry dough as directed in step I on page 168. Then roll the bottom piecrust and fit it into the pie pan following directions in step 4 on page 169. Spread the cooled cherry filling evenly in the piecrust. Dot with the butter. Prepare the top crust as directed in step 4 on page 169.

3. Freeze the pie for 10 minutes. Brush with the cream and sprinkle with the remaining I tablespoon sugar. Place the pie on a nonstick (gray, not black) baking sheet.

4. Bake 15 to 20 minutes on the bottom rack of the oven. Move the pie to the middle rack and bake until the crust is golden brown, 25 to 35 minutes. (Cover the crust with aluminum foil if it browns too quickly.) Remove from the oven and cool completely on a wire rack before cutting.

❋ Strawberry Pie with Whipped Cream

MAKES 8 SERVINGS

This luscious dessert with its bright red, shiny straw-berries looks like a work of art. The nutty cookie crumb crust—which also works for any no-cook pie filling—provides a crunchy contrast to the velvety strawberries.

CRUST
- 1 cup pecans or walnuts (whole or pieces)
- 2 tablespoons sugar
- ¾ cup crushed plain gluten-free cookies
- 2 tablespoons unsalted butter or buttery spread, at room temperature
- 1 teaspoon pure vanilla extract

FILLING
- 1 cup sugar
- 2 tablespoons cornstarch
- ⅛ teaspoon salt
- 1 cup cold water
- 2 tablespoons light corn syrup
- 4 tablespoons strawberry gelatin powder
- ½ teaspoon pure vanilla extract
- 1 drop red food coloring (optional)
- 1 quart fresh strawberries, hulled (about 4 cups)
- ¾ cup whipped topping

1. Place a rack in the middle of the oven. Preheat the oven to 325°F.

2. Make the crust: In a food processor, process the nuts and sugar until the nuts are finely ground. Add the cookies and process until they are finely ground. Add the butter and vanilla and process until the mixture is crumbly.

3. Press the crumbs evenly on the bottom and up the sides of a 9-inch round nonstick (gray, not black) pan. The edge of the crust should be level with the top of the pie pan. Use the bottom edge of a ¼-cup metal measuring cup to firmly press the crumbs where the bottom of the pan meets the side.

4. Bake until the crust smells fragrant and the edges of the crust just start to brown, 5 to 8 minutes. Cool the crust on a wire rack completely before adding the filling.

5. Make the filling: In a medium saucepan, whisk together the sugar, cornstarch, and salt until blended. Whisk in the water and cook over medium-high heat, whisking constantly, until the mixture is thick and clear, about 3 to 4 minutes. Remove from the heat and stir in the corn syrup, gelatin, vanilla, and food coloring, if using; cool completely, about 30 minutes.

6. Wash the strawberries, pat dry with paper towels, and then slice. Gently stir the strawberries into the cooled gelatin. Pour the filling into the prepared crust. Refrigerate until firm, about 3 to 4 hours.

7. Serve each slice of pie chilled or at room temperature, topped with 2 tablespoons of the whipped topping. Refrigerate the leftovers for up to 1 day.

Frozen Margarita Pie

MAKES 10 SERVINGS

The crunchy saltiness of the pretzel crust is a perfect complement to the sweet, smooth filling. These pies are perfect for adult dinner parties. For kids, omit the alcohol.

CRUST
4 ounces gluten-free pretzels
2½ tablespoons sugar
¼ cup (½ stick) unsalted butter or buttery spread, melted
¼ teaspoon salt (optional)

FILLING
1 (14- to 15-ounce) can sweetened condensed milk
3 tablespoons fresh lime juice
2 tablespoons fresh orange juice or orange liqueur
1½ tablespoons grated lime zest
1 tablespoon tequila (optional)
3 cups whipped topping
1 tablespoon grated lime zest, for garnish
1 whole lime, cut into 10 thin slices, for garnish
10 gluten-free pretzels, gently crushed, for garnish

1. Coat a 9-inch glass pie pan with cooking spray. Set aside.

2. Make the crust: In a food processor, process the pretzels and sugar until the pretzels are medium-size crumbs. Add the butter and salt, if using, and process. Press the crumbs onto the bottom and sides of the pie pan, then freeze 30 minutes.

3. Make the filling: In a clean food processor, combine the condensed milk, lime juice, orange juice, lime zest, and tequila, if using, and process until smooth. Set aside.

1. In a medium bowl, place 2 cups whipped topping. Gently fold in the margarita filling and then spread in the frozen pretzel crust. Return the pie to the freezer, uncovered, for 5 or 6 hours. Then wrap tightly in plastic wrap until serving time.

5. When ready to serve, let the pie sit at room temperature 10 minutes. Cut the pie into 10 slices. Garnish each slice with a tablespoon of the remaining cup of whipped topping, a dusting of grated lime zest, a slice of lime, and a sprinkle of crushed pretzels.

FROZEN MOJITO PIE

Replace the tequila and orange juice with 3 tablespoons white rum. Stir in 3 tablespoons finely chopped mint, plus use a few whole leaves for garnish.

Cherry Cobbler

MAKES 6 SERVINGS

Cobblers are American deep-dish fruit desserts, a variation of pies that are quick to make. Use this easy cobbler topping for other fruits such as apricots, peaches, or blueberries.

FILLING

- 6 cups pitted tart red cherries, drained thoroughly, reserving ¼ cup juice
- 1 teaspoon almond extract
- 1 cup sugar
- 4 teaspoons potato starch
- ⅛ teaspoon salt
- 1 tablespoon unsalted butter or buttery spread, melted

TOPPING

- 1 cup Carol's Sorghum Blend (page 14)
- ½ cup sugar plus 1 tablespoon, for sprinkling
- 1 teaspoon baking powder
- ½ teaspoon ground cinnamon
- ½ teaspoon xanthan gum
- ¼ teaspoon salt
- ¼ cup (½ stick) unsalted butter or buttery spread, melted, plus 1 tablespoon, for brushing
- 1 large egg, at room temperature
- 1 teaspoon grated lemon zest
- 1 teaspoon almond extract
- ⅓ cup buttermilk or Homemade Buttermilk (page 29), well shaken
- 2 tablespoons sliced almonds

1. Place a rack in the middle of the oven. Preheat the oven to 375°F. Generously grease an 8-inch square nonstick (gray, not black) baking dish.

2. Make the filling: In a medium bowl, toss the cherries with the reserved cherry juice and almond extract. Add the sugar, potato starch, and salt and toss until well combined; spread in the bottom of the prepared pan. Drizzle the melted butter over the fruit.

3. Make the topping: In the same bowl, whisk together the sorghum blend, ½ cup sugar, baking powder, cinnamon, xanthan gum, and salt. Beat in the melted butter, egg, lemon zest, almond extract, and buttermilk with an electric mixer on low speed, until just blended. Drop by tablespoonfuls on top of the cherries; the topping will spread as it bakes. Sprinkle with the remaining 1 tablespoon sugar and the sliced almonds.

4. Bake until the topping is lightly browned and crispy, 35 to 40 minutes. Cool the cobbler in the pan 5 minutes on a wire rack and then brush with the remaining 1 tablespoon melted butter. Cool another 15 minutes. Serve slightly warm.

FRESH PEACH COBBLER

In step 2, use the same amount of fresh peaches that have been peeled, pitted, and sliced into ¼-inch pieces. Reduce the sugar to ½ to ¾ cup, depending on the sweetness of the peaches.

☀ Apple Crisp

MAKES 6 SERVINGS

Juicy autumn apples and fragrant cinnamon make this dish enticing—and it's nutritious, too. You can also use pears in place of the apples.

FILLING

4 large apples of choice, unpeeled, cored, and thinly sliced (about 4 cups)
2 tablespoons golden or dark raisins
2 tablespoons packed light brown sugar
2 tablespoons cornstarch
½ teaspoon ground cinnamon
¼ teaspoon salt
2 tablespoons unsalted butter or buttery spread, at room temperature
2 tablespoons fresh lemon juice
2 tablespoons hot water (about 120°F)
1 tablespoon apple cider or apple juice (optional)
1 teaspoon pure vanilla extract

TOPPING

1 cup gluten-free rolled oats*
½ cup Carol's Sorghum Blend (page 14)
¼ cup finely chopped walnuts
2 tablespoons maple syrup, or more to taste
2 tablespoons unsalted butter or buttery spread, at room temperature
1 teaspoon pure vanilla extract
¼ teaspoon ground cinnamon
¼ teaspoon salt

1. Place a rack in the middle of the oven. Preheat the oven to 375°F. Generously grease an 8-inch microwave-safe baking pan.

2. Make the filling: In a medium bowl, toss the apples with the raisins, sugar, cornstarch, cinnamon, and salt until well blended. Add the butter, lemon juice, water, apple cider, and vanilla and mix thoroughly. Add to the prepared pan.

3. Cover the filling with wax paper. Microwave on high 5 minutes to soften the apples. (You may also cook this apple mixture in a saucepan over medium heat for 5 minutes.)

4. Make the topping: In a small bowl, blend the oats, sorghum blend, walnuts, maple syrup, butter, vanilla, cinnamon, and salt with your fingers until crumbly and sprinkle over the apples. Spray the topping with cooking spray.

5. Bake until the oat-crumble topping is crisp and the apples are tender, about 25 minutes. Cool the apple crisp in the pan on a wire rack 20 minutes. Serve slightly warm.

* Check with your physician before using gluten-free oats.

✺ Chocolate Fudge Espresso Pie

MAKES 12 SERVINGS

This delectable pie is like pure fudge, nestled on top of a chocolate-coffee crust. Dress it up for company with a few chocolate-covered espresso beans as a garnish, or replace the coffee with a tablespoon of your favorite liqueur, such as crème de menthe or Grand Marnier.

CRUST
- 1 package Pamela's Espresso Chocolate Chunk cookies (9 gluten-free espresso-chocolate cookies)
- 1 large egg, at room temperature

FILLING
- ¾ cup unsweetened natural or Dutch-process cocoa powder
- ½ cup (1 stick) unsalted butter or buttery spread, at room temperature
- 2 large eggs, at room temperature
- ½ cup sugar
- 1 teaspoon instant espresso or coffee powder
- 1 teaspoon pure vanilla extract
- ¾ cup whipped topping, for garnish
- 3 tablespoons cocoa nibs, for garnish (optional)

1. Place a rack in the middle of the oven. Preheat the oven to 350°F. Generously grease a 9-inch springform pan.

2. Make the crust: Place the cookies in a food processor. Process until thoroughly crushed. Add the egg and pulse until the mixture is thoroughly blended.

3. Press the mixture into the bottom of the prepared pan with your hands, covering it with plastic wrap to avoid sticking, if necessary. Remove the plastic wrap.

4. Make the filling: In a clean food processor combine the cocoa, butter, eggs, sugar, espresso powder, and vanilla. Process until thoroughly blended. Spread the filling in the crust, smoothing with a wet rubber spatula.

5. Bake until the filling starts to set around the edges and the crust browns, 15 to 20 minutes. Remove from the oven; the filling will continue to cook for a while. Cool on a wire rack for 30 minutes. Refrigerate for 2 hours before serving. Garnish with the whipped topping and cocoa nibs, if using.

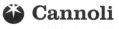 **Cannoli**

MAKES 16 CANNOLIS

Cannolis are Sicilian pastries and the word means "little tubes," aptly describing these fried pastry shells with a sweet creamy filling. Plan to eat the cannolis immediately after they're made. Cannoli tube forms are sold in sets of four in kitchen stores or online; it helps to have two sets of tubes to hasten the frying process.

FILLING
- 1 pound ricotta cheese (about 2 cups)
- ½ cup powdered sugar
- 1 tablespoon pure vanilla extract or Marsala
- 1 teaspoon grated orange zest

SHELLS
- 1 cup Carol's Sorghum Blend (page 14)
- ¾ cup tapioca flour
- ½ cup sweet rice flour
- 1 tablespoon granulated sugar
- 1 teaspoon xanthan gum
- 1 teaspoon guar gum
- ½ teaspoon salt
- ½ cup (1 stick) unsalted butter or buttery spread, at room temperature
- ⅓ cup milk of choice
- 1 tablespoon pure vanilla extract or Marsala
- Canola oil, for frying the shells
- Powdered sugar, for dusting the cannoli

1. Make the filling: Place the ricotta in a coffee filter–lined colander and drain overnight in the refrigerator. The next day, process the drained ricotta, sugar, vanilla, and orange zest in a food processor until smooth and then place in a heavy-duty freezer bag. Set aside.

2. Make the shells: In a food processor, process the sorghum blend, tapioca flour, rice flour, sugar, xanthan gum, guar gum, salt, and butter until crumbly. Add the milk and vanilla and process until the dough forms a ball. Remove the dough from the food processor and knead with your hands until smooth. Divide the dough in half and wrap half with plastic wrap, but do not refrigerate.

3. With a rolling pin, roll the remaining half of dough into a 12-inch square (about ¼ inch thick) between 2 pieces of heavy-duty plastic wrap. (Use a damp paper towel between the countertop and the plastic wrap to anchor the plastic wrap.) Remove the top layer of the plastic wrap and cut the dough into eight 4-inch squares.

4. Generously grease the cannoli tubes. Wrap a square of dough around each tube, pressing the edges together to seal.

5. In a heavy saucepan that is just big enough to hold one cannoli tube, heat 3 inches of oil to 350°F. With a slotted spatula, lower the tube into the hot oil and fry until the shells are golden brown, about 2 minutes. Lift them from the oil and drain on paper towels. When cooled, remove the shells from the tubes. Repeat with the remaining dough.

6. Cut ¼ inch from the corner of the freezer bag of the ricotta mixture and fill each shell with about 3 tablespoons of filling. Arrange the filled shells on a dessert plate and dust with powdered sugar. Serve immediately.

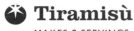

Tiramisù

MAKES 8 SERVINGS

Tiramisù means "pick me up" in Italian and its sweet, creamy texture is sure to give you a boost. Unlike traditional versions, we use shortbread cookies rather than ladyfingers, but the result is equally fantastic.

1 (8-ounce) package cream cheese or cream cheese alternative, softened
1 (8-ounce) container mascarpone cheese or cream cheese alternative, softened
¾ cup powdered sugar
2 cups whipped topping
½ cup very strong brewed coffee or espresso
2 tablespoons coffee liqueur
2 teaspoons pure vanilla extract
18 plain gluten-free cookies
2 tablespoons unsweetened Dutch-process cocoa powder
¼ cup gluten-free grated dark or milk chocolate, for garnish

1. Coat an 8-inch square baking pan with cooking spray. Set aside.

2. In a large bowl, beat together the cream cheese, mascarpone, and powdered sugar with an electric mixer on medium speed until thoroughly combined. With a rubber spatula, fold in a third of the whipped topping into the cheese mixture. Carefully fold in the remaining whipped topping.

3. In a shallow bowl, combine the coffee, coffee liqueur, and vanilla. Quickly and lightly dip each cookie in the coffee mixture only halfway. (Do not saturate the cookies or they will fall apart.) Place 9 cookies in a single layer on the bottom of the prepared pan. Spoon on half the cheese mixture and smooth it with a rubber spatula.

4. Dip the remaining cookies in the coffee mixture and arrange in a single layer on top of the cheese. Top with the remaining cheese and smooth it with a rubber spatula. Place the cocoa in a fine-mesh sieve and gently dust over the mascarpone.

5. Cover with plastic wrap and refrigerate at least 4 hours. (The flavor will be more fully developed if the tiramisù is chilled overnight.) Garnish each slice with a scant tablespoon of chocolate.

Sources
References and Information

You will find a great deal of helpful information from the following associations and organizations. I have worked with almost all of them in many capacities (client, customer, or partner) over the last fifteen years as we educate the world about the gluten-free lifestyle.

AllergyFree Passport
www.allergyfreepassport.com

American Academy of Allergy, Asthma & Immunology
www.aaaai.org

American Celiac Disease Alliance
www.americanceliac.org

American Dietetic Association
www.eatright.org

Asthma and Allergy Foundation of America
www.aafa.org

Autism Network for Dietary Intervention (ANDI)
www.autismndi.com

Autism Resource Network
www.autismshop.com

Autism Society
www.autism-society.org

Autism Speaks
www.autismspeaks.org

BIDMC Celiac Center at Harvard University
www.bidmc.org/celiaccenter

Bob & Ruth's Gluten-Free Dining & Travel Club
www.bobandruths.com

Case Nutrition Consulting
www.glutenfreediet.ca

Celiac Disease Center at Columbia University
www.celiacdiseasecenter.columbia.edu

Celiac Disease Clinic, Mayo Clinic Celiac Disease Research Program
www.mayoclinic.org/celiac-disease

Celiac Disease Foundation
www.celiac.org

Celiac Sprue Association/USA
www.csaceliacs.org

Clan Thompson's Celiac Site
www.celiacsite.com

Food Allergy & Anaphylaxis Network (FAAN)
www.foodallergy.org; www.fankids.org (for children)

GFreeCuisine
www.GfreeCuisine.com

Glutenfreeda
www.glutenfreeda.com

Gluten-Free Living Magazine
www.glutenfreeliving.com

Gluten-Free Certification Organization (GFCO)
www.gfco.org

Gluten-Free Works
www.glutenfreeworks.com

Gluten-Free Restaurant Awareness Program
www.glutenfreerestaurants.org

Gluten Intolerance Group of North America
www.gluten.net

Journal of Gluten Sensitivity
www.celiac.com

Living Without Magazine
www.livingwithout.com

National Foundation for Celiac Awareness (NFCA)
www.celiaccentral.org

National Institutes of Health
http://consensus.nih.gov/2004/
2004CeliacDisease118html.htm

National Jewish Health Center
www.njc.org

National Sorghum Producers
www.sorghumgrowers.com

Triumph Dining
www.triumphdining.com

University of Chicago Celiac Disease Center
www.celiacdisease.net

Center for Celiac Research & Treatment at MassGeneral for Children, Boston
www.celiaccenter.org

Ingredients

Amaranth
www.nuworldamaranth.com

Brown Rice
www.bobsredmill.com

Buckwheat
www.bobsredmill.com
www.thebirkettmills.com

Cornmeal (yellow)
www.bobsredmill.com
www.kinnikinnick.com

Hemp Seed
www.bobsredmill.com
www.nutiva.com

Montina
www.amazinggrains.com

Millet
www.bobsredmill.com

Oats
www.onlyoats.com
www.bobsredmill.com
www.creamhillstates.com
www.glutenfreeoats.com
www.giftsofnature.net

Potato Starch
www.bobsredmill.com

Quinoa
www.bobsredmill.com
www.ancientharvest.com

Rice Bran
www.bobsredmill.com
www.ener-g.com

Sorghum
www.authenticfoods.com
www.bobsredmill.com
www.twinvalleymills.com

Sweet Rice Flour
www.bobsredmill.com
www.ener-g.com

Tapioca
www.bobsredmill.com
www.ener-g.com

Teff
www.bobsredmill.com
www.teffco.com

Wild Rice
www.bobsredmill.com

Index

Page numbers in *italic* indicate photos